DOING OUR TIME ON THE OUTSIDE

One Prison Family of 2.5 Million

BARBARA ALLAN

Contact author at:
pfa.longisland@gmail.com

ISBN-13: 978-1981711789
ISBN-10: 1981711783

Cover and interior design:
The Publishing Pro, LLC,
Colorado Springs, Colorado

18j-c

DEDICATION

To prison families everywhere!

CONTENTS

FOREWORD

Almost fifty years ago, when faced with a traumatic life experience that most others hide from in undeserved shame and embarrassment, Barbara Allan had the fortitude to take the boldest of steps, publicly revealing the trauma she and her family endured when they became secondary victims of their loved one's crime and incarceration. In this book she opens the door even wider, allowing us a deeper understanding of the painful and often frightening private journey.

Barbara's was an exceptionally lonely journey, especially in the beginning. Yet she courageously pushed forward, persevering with the realization that while she felt very much alone, thousands of others were similarly affected and needed the same support and encouragement she so desperately needed but could not find anywhere. Instead of bemoaning her plight, she took the proverbial bull by the horns and established a meaningful support program for those living through the excruciating pain of the incarceration of a loved one. Today Barbara is the most experienced individual among us on all matters affecting prison families.

Barbara's long-ago vision of a program to encourage prison families became the desperately needed lighthouse for guiding a forgotten and even shunned population to the very support and resources they need to heal and succeed. Her program, Prison Families Anonymous, has also heightened public awareness to the fact that incarceration of one family member directly impacts the entire family system with far reaching consequences that can deteriorate the quality of life for entire communities.

For almost half a century Barbara Allan has boldly and lovingly persisted in her quest to improve the quality of life for families of incarcerated loved ones. Her tireless efforts have moved organizations and even entire communities to change attitudes and to publicly address the very painful and unique trauma experienced by millions of children and families of prisoners.

Those who are privileged to know Barbara personally have been consistently encouraged and enlightened by her wisdom, and uplifted by her indomitable spirit and amazing sense of humor; a trait she swiftly tells newcomers to the prison family they will need to successfully traverse their own challenging journeys.

Barbara Allan has courageously dedicated her life to embolden each of us to shed the cloak of anonymity and vigorously and publicly pursue true justice for all. The insight and love Barbara offers make this book a treasure expanding the bright light of the far-reaching beacon she initiated so long ago. It is a must-read treasure for anyone touched by incarceration.

With the greatest of love and respect,

—Carolyn Esparza, LPC
Founder and Chair
of the InterNational Prisoner's Family Conference

ACKNOWLEDGMENTS

This book was inside my head and heart for many years and might have stayed there forever if Erica Duncan had not invited me to a Herstory "Writing for Justice" workshop. She asked where I would want a stranger/reader to meet me, and I wrote the first few pages of this book.

Suzanne Jones read, edited, reread, typed, and retyped my words, always encouraging me. Without Sue's support, there would be no book.

Thank you Tina and Brenda for putting up with a mother who had an alternate (prison) family and might not always have been there for you.

Thanks to my mother and father, who kept us all sane and safe.

David Rothenberg, my mentor and my friend, thank you for almost fifty years of being there for me.

Thank you, Shirley C. Anytime I needed to be anywhere, you were always willing to accompany me, drive me, and offer me a hand.

ONE
Not Me (1968)

I took out the double stroller and put Tina in the back and Brenda in the front. It was forty minutes after leaving the Nassau County Jail, forty-five minutes after my visit with their father, my husband, Gene.

I hoped the guard would allow him to look out onto Carman Avenue and get a glimpse of his girls. This was our once-a -week ritual since Gene had been arrested a year earlier. We knew that he would soon be transferred to an upstate prison, where our routine would have to change.

How strange what eventually seems familiar. Going to the county jail twice a week was now pro forma. I knew the route; it was twenty minutes from the home we had shared and where the girls and I still lived.

I knew the guards, and they knew and trusted me. They might have even liked me. I had gotten used to seeing Gene behind a Plexiglas window and speaking through a phone, discussing intimate details with someone to my left, someone to my right, and the knowledge that someone else might be listening to those calls. It wasn't okay, but it was accepted.

Tina and Brenda had not had any contact with their father for more than year, not since a week before he was charged with murder.

No one under the age of sixteen could visit at the Nassau County Jail. The girls were two-and-a-half and three-and-a-half. They could not speak to him or hear his voice; phone calls home were not permitted. They could not read his letters. The words were squiggly designs on a legal pad that meant nothing to them. It was up to me to keep him alive in their minds. But did I want to? Should I?

As we left the jail to head home, I felt exhausted. On that day it was just my girls and me. Marjorie was usually with me. Dear Marjorie, a coworker, was barely an acquaintance. After hearing about the terrible event, she packed a suitcase and told me that she would be staying with me for a while.

"You will need help with the girls and here I am," she said.

And there she was indeed. I leaned on her both physically and emotionally. Sometimes my knees shook, and I didn't think I could make it from the parking lot to the street.

These outings with Marjorie occurred after my visits with Gene, visits that were draining, frustrating, and just plain sad. There was a routine. I would walk into the processing room, where Walter greeted the visitors. Of all the guards and correction officers I would run into over the years, Walter was the least intimidating and the kindest. How grateful I am that my first experience at a jail had Walter as the visiting room "receptionist." I was so frightened the first time I walked into that room that I went through the initial processing like a robot. As I recall, Walter looked at my driver's license, told me to leave my belongings, including all jewelry, in an assigned locker. I think they allowed me to wear my wedding band. I don't remember if they wanded me or if they had a metal detector, as they do now. Much of those days are still a blur. I am more aware of the feelings than I am of the actual events.

I do remember that one of the officers called up to the tier and told them that the inmate, Herman Gene Allan, had a visitor, and then I was finally allowed to go through the first set of gates. When those gates clanged shut behind me, I jumped and felt my heart beating so hard I thought it was going to explode. My body was shaking, and I could barely catch my breath. After the first gates closed I was left—for what must have been seconds, though it seemed much longer—trapped inside a cage. Finally, they opened the second set of gates, and I could see into a large room with stools facing a wall, Plexiglas, and a telephone receiver. I sat on the assigned small stool, waiting for Gene to come in through the inmates' door. After waiting what seemed an eternity, Gene appeared. He was strip-searched before and after each time we met, the humiliating price he would pay to be allowed a visit.

He took his seat on the opposite side of the Plexiglas. We each picked up a phone receiver and tried to have a natural conversation, aware that every word we said was possibly being listened to or recorded. The scattered bits of conversations from others were background noises as we tried to speak. I had so many questions. There was so much that I did not understand. Also, there were practical concerns. I was left with a house we had purchased only six months before. There were unpaid and unanticipated bills, insurance papers to deal with, leaks and creaks in the house. I was overwhelmed. I didn't believe that I could survive all this on my own.

TWO
Why Me? (1968)

Immediately after his arrest, Gene was brought to the Nassau County Medical Center jail ward, known at that time as Meadowbrook Hospital. It all felt surreal. Carol Weinstein, a friend from elementary school, had recently graduated from law school. She, my mother, and I braved the reporters parked outside the hospital and tried to get in to see him. My mother threw her coat over my head so that the photographers would not get a head shot, and we ran the gauntlet, raw emotion permeating. The press was relentless. The news coverage was all over the place, with so many inaccuracies. One headline said that Gene had killed his father, a colonel in the National Guard. This added to the indignity. *My* father was the colonel. Gene's father had never seen service, unless you include community service that had been imposed by the courts.

All day long people called to express sympathy for the death of *my* father.

My father was a well-respected member of the Hempstead community. He had a small TV-repair business in town; he was active in veteran affairs and town politics. Archie Pugatz had an impeccable reputation as a gregarious person. Both he and my mother were active in the local synagogue. My mother played Mah Jong every Friday night.

They were known and liked by everyone who knew them. Nothing in their lives had prepared them for this.

We made it to the hospital and were escorted into a room, where I saw a shackled stranger with two black eyes, head bandaged, lying in a hospital bed, unable to raise his head to look at me. His guards would not allow me to remain for more than a few minutes. For that I felt a rush of gratitude. I ran out of there blinded by tears, only wanting to go home to my children to get away from the nightmare.

The hospital stay was a short one, and I never went back.

And so, on to the jail.

I went alone that first time.

I remember the cigarette machine in the lobby. I could purchase packs of cigarettes for Gene, only if I had the exact change. (Years later, Prison Families Anonymous was invited to be in that area of the visiting room. They let us in, as an agency, to comfort and help visitors navigate the system. We kept a cigar box filled with change for the cigarette machine.)

At the time, we were allowed to bring a package of food. Fruit was seldom served to the inmates, so I would stop on the way to the visit and pick up some fresh fruit for him. That practice was continued until someone supposedly injected alcohol, or some such contraband, into a plum. At that point, probably forty years ago, no outside food items were allowed, though money was acceptable so that our inmates could buy items in the commissary.

That first time, I wanted to scream an unending shriek. I wanted to cry hysterically and run from there. I did not want to be there! I could not possibly be in a jail visiting room.

Instead, I quietly asked him, "How was your day?"

I was fighting back tears. I gave in to a flood of questions and news bits.

"What did they give your for breakfast? Was it edible?"

"Dr. Triola [my principal] called a last minute faculty meeting."

"Brenda has a cough."

And yes, "Why did you do it, Gene? How could you do this to us? Oh, and by the way, I need to pay Mr. Schatz [our lawyer] before our next court date."

"I love you. Help me! Please help me." I mustn't cry because if I did, I might never stop.

We were two scared people, clinging to a boat, looking for life preservers.

Of course I held on. How could I not? The hysteria settled down to a familiar emotion.

As soon as the shock wore off and reality hit, my father called a colleague of his. Both men were active in the National Guard and knew each other socially and through their service. George Schatz was the only practicing attorney any of us knew. His specialty was real-estate transactions.

George might never have handled a criminal case, but he cared about me. He was aware of the domestic violence and was concerned about the safety of my family. He called upon a friend and colleague who did have experience in practicing criminal law. The two attorneys agreed to defend Gene.

Our lawyers were our life preservers. They were the most important people in the universe because their ability, or lack thereof, would determine our future. When George asked for a retainer, without a second thought, I endorsed my paycheck over to him. I would just have to manage to get by until the next payday.

I paid Gene's legal fees in dribs and drabs, going into the few resources I had, with the help of my parents, who stood by me no matter what the consequences. I knew that we would always have food on the table, but it was scary. Not only was I in debt to the attorneys, I had lost Gene's income. Me, who always paid my bills the day they were due.

THREE
The New Normal (1967)

The seasons changed. I bundled the children up for their walks or dressed them in tee shirts. He could barely see them anyway. From his vantage point in the jail, he saw some movement down below, but he could not discern their little faces. The walks became less frequent. We had birthdays, Mother's Day, Father's Day, a wedding anniversary. Life moved on. But our time was measured by court dates, visiting days, and the never ending fear of not knowing how this would end. I lived one day at a time without being aware that this was how I was surviving.

I still had no answers. I knew the facts, but there were too many missing pieces.

The attorneys were trying to work out a viable defense for Gene. He had been charged with first-degree murder. The attorneys initially considered an insanity defense. The insanity defense was tough to prove; the trial would be expensive and lead to even more publicity. If found guilty, Gene would be sent to Mattawan, an upstate facility for the criminally insane. Not a particularly desirable option. Also, there would be no end date. It was a gamble.

We did not ask for bail. Our concern was that if he were released on bail, he might continue to be a threat—this time to us.

The only psychiatrists he saw in the county jail were court-appointed, intended to judge his mental state, or defense-appointed, intended to rebut any diagnosis that might prove harmful to our case. No one ever offered him therapy or counseling or even asked him how he felt about what he did. And so he sat in a jail cell, reading novels, obsessing about his fate, not dealing with the demons or the reality of what he had done. He just never spoke of it.

I was living in the shadow of those demons. I frantically called our psychiatrist and begged him to assure me that my daughters would not suffer the same affliction as their father and grandfather. There were no guarantees. I cried myself to sleep night after night, but I had no idea for whom I was crying.

Tina and Brenda were aware that something was wrong. Where had their daddy disappeared? Did they do something to chase him away? I tried to allay their fears and answer their questions honestly. "Daddy did something wrong. He needs to be punished for what he did. When you do something you should not do, you know that Mommy or Grandma might give you a time-out. It does not mean that we do not love you. Daddy is so sorry that he cannot be here with you for now. Grown-up time-outs just last a little longer."

We would lie on the bed, Tina holding tightly to Rory, her stuffed lion. She would look up at me with those big questioning brown eyes, making my heart melt. Tina was the thoughtful one, retreating to her "thinking tree" if she needed space. She was always the big sister and the protector.

Brenda, holding her pacifier in her mouth with strong determination, was seeking security in the only way she knew. She sensed that everything was *not* all right, and if she needed to hold onto something, so be it. Gene was always upset that Brenda still needed a pacifier, but now he had no vote.

Brenda was the strong-willed child, the girl who as a toddler climbed to the top of the monkey bars and looked down at her sister and me with defiance, her demeanor saying, "See, I can do anything. I am not afraid."

Tina would grab my arm and say, "Mommy, I'm afraid. Make her come down. She's going to fall."

Brenda did not fall, and Tina never did stop worrying about her sister.

How I wished that I had the appropriate words or the magic pill to make this all go away for us. I would have been grateful to just have the energy to hug them a little longer. I told them it was okay to cry if they really felt sad, and I let them see me cry—but only for a little while. Eventually we would all fall asleep.

This did not happen all in one night but gradually as situations dictated and questions were asked.

We were not going to fall into an abyss of sorrow.

And so the year went by, with all the ups and downs of a Coney Island roller coaster.

I was sleeping on the couch every night, when I could finally fall asleep with the help of Prozac.

FOUR
Not Me, Gene (1966)

On the night of the murder Gene had called me at my parents' house.

"Barbara, I did it. I did it. I shot my father. He's dead, Barbara." And then he broke down, and his words became inaudible.

"Where are you? Tell me where you are."

"I'm home. I'm home. I'm in the kitchen. He's dead on the floor. Barbara, I shot him."

I visualized my kitchen. I saw the phone on the wall. I knew how the cord would dangle as he paced while speaking to me. I pictured blood on my linoleum, the brown corner bench, the color-coordinated refrigerator, avocado— very sixties but now saturated with the clashing color, the bright red of blood. I quickly shook my head, forcing myself back to reality. Unbelieving, I returned to the surreal conversation.

I said that I did not believe him. He was certainly not above lying to manipulate me into returning to him. "Listen," he said as he placed the phone to the mouth of his dying father. I heard the gurgling sound of death.

Gene and his father, Herman, had gone out bar cruising. In some gin mill in town, Gene got into a fight with another drunk. The reason doesn't matter. A word or a gesture, ill perceived, could unleash the beast. It was not the first time his aggression had been let loose on someone besides me. But this opponent had a knife, and he used it to slash Gene between his thumb and forefinger, causing a fountain of blood to spurt out and Gene to be distracted. In that moment of distraction, he gave his opponent the opportunity to smash him in the face, causing him to fall and hit his head, knocking him out. We later found out that this caused a concussion.

When he came to, still not subdued, he looked for his father and couldn't find him. He staggered out into the street, still blind with rage and bleeding from various cuts. He saw that Herman had retreated and was outside the bar, casually leaning against the car. Once again his father did not have his back. The rage intensified. The assailant who conquered him was no longer his focus. Instead he centered his fury on the father who had sadistically mistreated him throughout his childhood and once again disappointed him.

The pain he was feeling now was indistinguishable from the old pains, the pain of having his hands held over a lit stove as punishment for a childhood transgression. The humiliation of being beaten in a barroom brawl was equated with the humiliation he felt at being made to wear a dress to his first-grade class, because he had displeased his father.

Head throbbing, bleeding profusely, but with an adrenaline surge, Gene got into the car and, by the grace of the powers-that-be, they were able to maneuver the short distance home.

As they walked into the empty house, Herman suggested that Gene go to the hospital. But, first things first! They found their way to the liquor in the kitchen cabinet and continued arguing about Herman deserting Gene. Words got louder and gestures became more threatening. Gene blamed his father for interfering in his marriage and accused him of being the catalyst that caused me to leave him.

A glass shattered on the kitchen floor. Herman bent to pick up the pieces. For some reason this seemed ludicrous to Gene. The broken glass, the bleeding, the pounding in his head, the desertion were all coming together into a crescendo.

Gene was blacking out, reality flashing on and off, sometimes like a blinking neon light and other times as if someone was playing with a light switch.

He left the kitchen, walked through the dining room, turned into the living room, and made one more turn into the den. He opened the closet door, retrieved a rifle, followed the same path back to the kitchen, leaving the den, going into the living room, turning into the dining room and returning to the kitchen where his father was picking up slivers of glass, between sips of whiskey. He pointed the rifle at his father, who looked stunned when he realized what Gene had in his hand. Herman's final words were "Not me, Gene."

Gene pulled the trigger and watched the man who had molded him fall to the floor and die amidst the remaining broken glass.

As he revealed this on the phone, my knees buckled. I think I might have blacked out for a second. I could barely breathe. Instinctively, I screamed for my own father, who was lying peacefully in bed next to my mother.

If I knew nothing else, I knew that our world would never be the same again.

I must have muttered something to Gene about calling the police because he told me they were on the way. And then I heard the faint sound of sirens seeping through the phone receiver. I sat paralyzed until my father called my name.

Immediately after the murder the police came to my parents' home to interview us. It was probably four or five in the morning by then. They respectfully questioned me. I was still in shock; the adrenaline was surging through me, and I felt that I had nothing to hide. The officers seemed friendly and sympathetic; I answered honestly and was very forthright. It never entered my mind that I should stop babbling and ask for a lawyer.

I called Terry, our babysitter, and asked her to take the children home with her.

FIVE
It's the Guns (1966)

Terry knew about the insanity in the Allan household. She had experienced the wrath of Gene three days before the murder. Terry, as usual, had arrived to care for the children so that I could leave for work. In his still drunken stupor, hungover from the night before, Gene had decided that I should not go to work and that was supposed to be that. I ignored his command. He insisted that Terry leave. She refused. She had a responsibility toward the children, and it was apparent to her that something was wrong.

Something was indeed wrong. I felt as though I had just awakened from a nightmare. I was still stunned from the goings on of the night before. I was not as lucid as I should have been; I was still not thinking rationally. I had not slept all night and was in a state of disbelief. The only thing I knew for sure was that my children needed a safe haven and that I had to go to work. There were thirty second-graders waiting for me, and it was too late to call for a substitute. I wanted to go on with my day. I needed to feel normal.

Feeling normal would be a stretch, after what happened the night before.

Gene and Herman were in the den, peacefully playing cards. After tucking my babies in for the night, I decided to go to a nearby supermarket and do the week's grocery shopping, secure that the two men would listen for the girls. Little Miss Pollyanna did not factor in that there was beer and booze in the house.

When I returned home, I needed help to unload the groceries. That was Gene's job. He would usually be listening for the car and come right out to help me. Carrying the lighter packages, I opened the front door to call for Gene. I heard a screaming baby. Leaving my groceries on the kitchen counter, I started up the stairs to Brenda's bedroom. Gene called after me to stop.

"Leave her alone! You spoil her rotten! For God's sake, woman, let her cry."

Uh-oh! My knees buckled. I recognized the slurring voice. My heart beat faster, and I went into panic mode. I had been gone for maybe two hours, and Dr. Jekyll had turned into Mr. Hyde.

He followed me up the stairs, commanding me to let my baby cry. Of course, I would not stop, and he could not allow me to disobey his drunken commands. He would lose face in front of his equally intoxicated father. The yelling got louder, the crying continued, and I tried to soothe my baby by holding her against my loudly thumping heart. With all the commotion Tina woke up, and both girls were now crying in unison.

I had defied Gene, and he got angrier and angrier. He lost his self-control and was blind with rage. When I refused to back down, he returned to the den where Herman waited. In retrospect, I realize that he needed to go back to the bottle that was waiting down there.

I still needed to put the groceries away, make sure that both girls had calmed down, and get my clothes and briefcase ready for school. I proceeded out of habit, not feeling, not thinking, and stuffing all that had transpired down into my soul. I had a sense that my responses were irrational, but everything was out of focus.

Sometime amidst all the ranting and raving, Gene must have gone out to the car for the groceries, because I found them sitting on the counter next to the ones I had brought in. That is the craziness I lived with. Everything quieted down. I put the groceries in the proper places, stopped shaking, and went to our bedroom.

Craving rest and knowing that the next day I needed to be refreshed and able to deal with my second-graders, I lay down in bed, closed my eyes, and appreciated the silence. Had they both, perhaps—please, God—passed out downstairs?

But no, the respite did not last long. I smelled him before I heard or saw him. The door opened and the odor of whiskey and tobacco nauseated me. He lay down, touching me, trying to arouse me. This was not the man I had deeply loved, the man whose caresses had, at one time, caused my whole body to respond with fierce desire. This was a drunken bully who did not belong in my bed.

I pushed him away. This infuriated him. The last straw! He staggered to the door, locked it, and went to his dresser. He opened a drawer and took out a gun. I was shocked. I had no idea that he had hidden a gun in the house we shared with two toddlers. He aimed it at me, but when it went off, the barrel was facing downwards, and it exploded into the floorboards. I screamed for Herman to help me. He did not respond, but the sound of the gunshot must have cleared Gene's head. He came out of his drunken haze a little and passed out on our bed, allowing me the opportunity to escape into the children's room. I held them tightly, praying for morning and waiting until I felt it was safe to go into our room again. If he did wake up, I did not want him looking for me in their room. I heard movement from Herman and knew that the bullet did not hit him.

I did not gather the girls and run out of the house. I was paralyzed with fear. I did not call the police. I knew that I needed to call someone, to reach out for help. I was so immobilized that I did nothing. I have no excuse—except that I thought if I left, or if he woke while I was dialing the phone, he just might shoot me. As long as he was in that drunken passed-out sleep, I was a little less afraid. The night passed without another sound from him, and morning finally came.

I prepared for work as though nothing was amiss.

SIX
Family Court (1966)

But by golly, Gene, always the pragmatic one, did do something.

That was the morning Gene called the police to evict Terry. He did not want her to take the children. He did not want me to go to work.

Terry refused to leave me alone with him; she was there when the Hempstead police responded to Gene's call.

Gene's demeanor flipped 360 degrees. It was, "Yes, Officer. Of course, Officer. I am sure that you understand how emotional women get. My wife is always so dramatic. We were just having a little disagreement. Terry was butting in. Since she does not live here, I don't want her in my house."

Gene's eyes were red, and he was still slurring and smelled of alcohol. I am sure that I looked terrified. I was on the brink of hysteria

With everything going on around me, my biggest concern at that moment was who would take care of my second-grade class. I had not called in for a substitute

I don't care what the common theory is but, in my experience, insanity is a contagious disease. And I caught it from my husband!

The officers rightly appraised the situation.

One officer escorted Gene out of the room while another

stayed with me. He suggested that Terry leave with the children and that I go right to Family Court to obtain an order of protection.

This was 1966. Oprah and Dr. Phil must have still been in elementary school. It was years before OJ Simpson went on trial for the murder of Nicole Simpson. No one talked about domestic violence. It was kept locked away behind closed doors, just like the funny uncle who talked to himself and was locked in the attic.

The mentality back then was that if anyone in the neighborhood was beaten by her spouse, she probably had it coming anyway. Call the cops and they would usually take the abuser for a walk around the block and tell him to go easy on the little woman. Meanwhile, the victim was urged to forgive and forget. It was, after all, just a marital spat.

It must have looked really serious to our first responders for them to suggest taking a more drastic step. The police waited while I phoned my parents, who came right over. They did not leave until the children left with Terry and I was safely out of the house.

My mother, father, and I went into the menacing-looking courthouse. We were clinging to each other, each of us with shaking knees.

Near the entrance, there was an intake desk where I spoke to a clerk. It was difficult to hold my hand steady enough to fill out the required forms. Then we had to sit in a waiting area until we were called into an office to be interviewed by an intake officer. I had no idea who these people were, what their authority was, if they were peace officers or social workers. I just did as I was told.

After listening to my rambling story of what happened the night before, I was told that a subpoena was going to be issued for Gene to appear in Family Court and that I would be given an emergency order of protection. I chuckled. I will now have a piece of paper to protect me. I supposed it was better than nothing. It did give me a sense of control, if not a feeling of security, but it was not a shield or a bulletproof vest.

A subpoena to get Gene into court wasn't necessary. Before I had a chance to complete all the paperwork, there he was, disheveled and manic, looking for his wife. First yelling and cursing and then crying, "Where is Barbara? Please. I love her. Please let me talk to my wife. I love you, Barbara. Come home with me. I am sorry if I did anything to scare you. Just come home." And then he started sobbing and begging some more. You know there was the part of me that wanted to put my arms around him and console him. Of course, I instantly shook that feeling.

As security tried to calm him down, it was very strongly suggested that I take my children and leave our home. I objected, saying that if I left, he could say that I deserted him, and he would be allowed to retain possession of our home. Such were the laws back then.

"Do not go back, and do not worry about your house. That is the least of your worries," I was told emphatically. "Take your children and find a safe place to go. A house is replaceable. Your children's mother is not."

Go someplace safe? And where would that be? Domestic violence shelters were nonexistent back then. There was no social worker to advise me, no one to suggest an alternative living space, and no one to mention Al-Anon. Just go and God bless.

They did hold Gene in a conference room, allowing us a safe exit. We scooted out of there as quickly as we could, not sure how much time we had.

We made it back to my house, quickly packed a few necessities, and went home with my parents. They lived four blocks from 10 Foster Place in Hempstead, the address of our dream house. This was certainly the first place that Gene would look for me, but he was warned to keep away from me, and now I had a piece of paper to protect us. I sure hoped that paper was bulletproof. The thought was not very reassuring.

SEVEN
My Day in Court (1966)

And that is how, two days later, I was able to receive the phone call in the middle of the night telling me that a murder had been committed in my kitchen and how it came to pass that there were three police officers sitting in my parents' living room in the middle of the night.

I had seen signs of a deteriorating mind throughout our marriage. I called Gene my Jekyll and Hyde. At that time I was not privy to all the chaos in Gene's childhood. I knew that my father-in-law had a checkered past, and I knew that their relationship was rocky, but I had no frame of reference to understand the dynamics of a lifetime of dysfunction and abuse.

So there they were. Three police officers waiting for what I would say. Gene had confessed, and I knew there was nothing to hide. I spoke candidly to the responding officers, and answered all their questions as honestly as I could; I just kept right on talking. I told about the domestic violence, about the drinking, and about the relationship Gene had with his father. I didn't know when to shut up.

I admitted that the first thing I did after "the call" was to wake up my parents. As they were trying to calm me down and find out what had happened, I told them that Gene had killed his father. I hysterically repeated the conversation I just had with Gene.

Because I admitted that I had told a third party what was said, I would not be granted the right to invoke the law of privileged communication. If you ever watched any of the old James Cagney law-and-order movies, you heard the offender say to his girlfriend and confidante, "Let's get married." It was not a loving proposal but a then-you-can't-testify-against-me tactic.

Me and my big mouth. During the pre-trial proceedings I was subjected to more than two hours on the witness stand—just to determine if I would be required to appear as a witness against my husband. I had to go back and revisit the "night in question." Yes, I broke the bond of privilege by confiding in a third party. However this was an utterance proclaimed while I was in a state of shock.

"What did you say to them?"

"I honestly don't remember. Nothing seemed real. It was like a dream and I was not sure what was happening."

"What did they say to you?"

"They were asking what was wrong and if I was okay. Their concern was for me, and they were trying to calm me down."

I am not sure why, but the judge ruled in my favor. I was spared the agony of having to testify for the prosecution.

Meanwhile, Gene continued to be held without bail.

Sometime after the murder, my mother and Terry went to my house to arrange for the cleanup of the blood and whatever other remnants remained of that night. I was spared the actual sight, but I still see it vividly in my imagination.

EIGHT
The Rebel (the 1950s)

I was the only child of adoring parents. My extended family was loving and accepting.

There *was* a great uncle. "Shhh, Uncle Al drinks a little too much."

And then we heard some whispers about Freddie, a second cousin. He was a little strange because, it was explained, he was a "change of life" baby.

Mostly, though, nothing suggested where my story would go. Both sides of the family intermingled. We all lived in the same ghetto in the Bronx, New York. As a tribe, we celebrated happy occasions, mourned losses, appreciated each other's successes. If anyone was in need, someone was always there with words of encouragement or with a couple of dollars "to tide you over."

I never heard a curse word from family. No one ever laid a hand on me in anger. Alcohol was available to toast triumphs and to celebrate holidays. A little wine was necessary at Passover. Beer was the beverage of choice on hot summer days.

It was not unusual, in this culture, for us to be brainwashed with the idea that girls would continue their education until they got their Mrs. Degree. Meanwhile, we would study for a job as a teacher or a nurse. Or perhaps go to Katherine Gibbs Secretarial School, where we would be taught the art of typing and serving coffee to the boss, always a man, while wearing white gloves and a perky little hat.

Not me!

I was going to seek a career in journalism. My mother pooh-poohed that idea. "Really, Barbara, where do you think that majoring in journalism will take you? Do you want to be an English teacher? Be practical. You can always write as a hobby but as a profession? Well, you need to choose something more realistic."

No, I did not want to teach high-school English. If I was destined to teach, I wanted to be able to nurture young children. So I quit college for a year, fell passionately in love with Howard, switched my major, and three years later received my BS in elementary education.

I also learned a hard lesson in relationships. I loved Howard in a way that transcended logic. I would never love anyone else with that intensity, probably not even Gene. But alas, Howard treated me shabbily, over and over again, eroding whatever confidence I had. I was looking for validation from Howard, the man who would not take my virginity because I was special. The Madonna and whore way of looking at sexuality did not do a lot for my ego. I would much rather have been loved than worshipped.

I met Howard the summer before I was to start college. My cousin Norma and I went to Asbury Park, New Jersey, to work for the summer, my first time away from home. And there he was: my hard drinking, gambling, handsome, blue-eyed mentor. I learned many a life's lesson from Howard Trout, particularly that I was disposable. For six summers, I returned to my job in Convention Hall, on the boardwalk, dispensing milkshakes and sandwiches at Steve's Snack Bar and trying to will Howard to love me just a little bit more. In September, it was back home, completing college and eventually beginning a teaching career. My summers were spent back in New Jersey, with some time allotted to Provincetown, Massachusetts, back then a flourishing art community.

My school friend, Connie, and I shuffled back and forth from New York in my little Nash Metropolitan. P-town, as we referred to it, was an extension of "the Village." Artists, writers, and musicians found their way to the Cape to mingle with the fishermen and largely Portuguese population.

Nothing was off limits as we walked the streets barefoot, going from bar to bar where I modeled for the budding artists and paid for the portraits with my poetry. Jazz was the dominant music during that phase of my life, and my favorite non-country musician was Miles Davis.

My experiences in both communities were preparing me for what was yet to come.

My first exposure to a jail cell was in Asbury Park, the night of Teddy's accident. We were out celebrating, mourning the end of the summer. I was going home in a few days to start my semester of student teaching. Howie was working; we were going to meet him later, so it was Teddy, Art, Richie, and me,

We were in a jovial mood, after a night of drinking. Ted

did not see the couple as they left a bar; they stepped off the sidewalk and walked between parked cars, right into the path of our car. There was one fatality. An instant death.

My memory is a little blurry, but I do remember the police bringing us all to the local precinct where we gathered in a jail cell. None of us, back in 1957, was familiar with the terms DWI or DUI. They did not bring out a breathalyzer. The incident was treated as an accident, and no charges were filed. Teddy's blond hair turned gray almost overnight. I never felt the same way about driving again. Whenever I got into a car after that night, I was a little bit wary.

The accident might have tempered my driving, but it didn't stop us from drinking. Eighteen was the legal drinking age in New York, and I took advantage of alcohol's availability. As a self-proclaimed weekend beatnik, I joined the excitement of the Greenwich Village scene during the late fifties and early sixties. I was trying to find my place as a young woman in a changing world. And the world was changing. It was an exciting time to be alive.

To the dismay of my parents, every Friday at the end of the school day, I packed an overnight bag, left suburbia behind, shed my identity, and transformed into rebel me. The drug culture was alive and well; all kinds of people were asserting their rights to be who they were, gay or straight. The civil rights movement was happening. Women were no longer going to accept being treated as an underclass. A woman's place was in the House—and the Senate. Free love was everyone's motto. We didn't trust anyone over thirty. And I needed to prove that I was desirable.

My school chum and Provincetown companion, Connie, had a room on Hudson Street, where I was welcome to crash on weekends while trying to ignore the roaches and all who entered there. My drug of choice was scotch, and my artistic outlet was writing poetry.

After I started teaching, I brought my adventurous spirit around the world. I no longer hung out in Asbury Park, waiting for Howie to love me. Instead of losing my inhibitions in Provincetown, I discovered the west bank of Paris, the east side of London, the Trevi Fountain in Rome, and the excitement of traveling the world with a Euro pass, a bottle of wine, and *Europe on 5 Dollars a Day* tucked in my backpack.

In the summer of 1959, I traveled with Lois Lipsky. We visited much of Europe. We were two young elementary school teachers who were anxious to take on anything that came our way. The experience was so invigorating that I went back the following summer with another teacher friend, Helen. My appetite to be a part of the world was not yet sated.

We went to the Salzburg Festival in Austria. We slept in a Volkswagen when we found that the hotel we booked in advance did not save our room. We hitched a ride from Yugoslavia to Italy because the trains were unreliable. We sneaked across Checkpoint Charlie from West to East Berlin, because Helen spoke Russian and we wanted to talk to the Russian border guard. I water-skied in Barcelona—even though I do not know how to swim.

I was afraid of nothing and I loved the excitement of facing the unexpected.

It was amazing fun, two summers of living like a vaga-
bond, with no plans other than to go wherever the spirit
took us.

Come September I returned to teaching and had to be
satisfied with my weekends in the Village.

NINE
We Both Loved Country Music (circa 1963)

A month after returning to the United States, I met Gene. He inadvertently discovered Louie's, "our bar" on 4th Street near Bleeker. This was my home away from home. It was all happening right in this neighborhood. We lived it and loved it.

Gene had just been discharged from the army. The military base was over the bridge in New Jersey, and the first thing he did after obtaining his freedom was to seek out the excitement of New York City.

It was a Friday night, and I walked into Louie's. We were going to a party uptown and were waiting for all the troops to arrive. Connie pulled me aside.

"See that cute guy sitting alone near the end of the bar? I was talking to him. He just got out of the army, and he spotted you as you came in. He asked me if I would introduce him to you. I invited him to go to the party with us."

I smiled. He really was good looking. "Sure," I said. There was no one special in my life at the moment. Joseph, whom I had been dating for a few years, had just asked me to help him obtain a divorce from his wife who was still living in Yugoslavia, so I felt no loyalty there.

The party was fun. There was plenty of alcohol and pot. Gene was drinking, but so was I—and everyone else. It was what we did. Gene did not leave my side.

It wasn't a Howie kind of love. But there was a spark; there was a hint of passion; there was the sense of something dangerous, an unknown quality that attracted me. Because we met, he decided to stay in New York and was able to rent a studio apartment.

We were together as often as possible. We went to the movies, out for ice cream sundaes, and to the honky-tonks for country music. For the first time I was dating a man who shared my taste in music. I finally found another person who loved the songs that Hank Williams sang. I had no doubt that he was my soul mate.

We did the things that people do as they try to get to know each other. Gene came to my parents' home on Long Island, and I played at being domestic, wearing an apron and cooking dinner for us. On weekends I met him in the city, where we partied, and felt free. He gave me a copy of *The Rubaiyat of Omar Khayyam*. We read and wrote poetry. We drank in all the bars and clubs scattered throughout Greenwich Village in the early sixties. Here we listened to Bob Dylan and Joan Baez. I was introduced to *The Three Penny Opera*, my favorite show to this day. We had no idea what would happen to us when we grew up. And frankly we didn't care. We were having fun.

Gene was living off his military separation pay and working part time in an industry just becoming prominent. He taught himself the art of programming computers.

As he felt more comfortable with me, Gene dropped his guard. His paranoia started to show.

One night we went to Louie's. We left early and went to Gene's apartment. He continued to drink until he became maudlin. "Go home, leave me alone. Why are you here? I met someone else. I don't want you here." His eyes looked dilated and his words were slurred. Then he started crying. "Just go. Just get the hell out of my life. You're too damn good for me."

Truer words were never spoken. I didn't take his good advice. Instead, I felt as though I was being tossed aside again.

I slinked away back to my home on the Island, took the phone off the hook, thinking that he might try to reach me, and I did not want to deal with any more drama. I also did not want the phone to wake my parents.

At around three in the morning, there was a series of loud knocks on the front door. The Hempstead Police had gotten a call from a man stating that he could not reach me. He was afraid I might have harmed myself.

I felt vindicated. He did not throw me away. And I thought I was in love! We went to the corner bar and made the decision that this was the perfect time to get married.

We eloped to Maryland where, on January 9, 1964, a Justice of the Peace married us.

Gene had been married for a short time while living in DC and we needed to get a copy of his divorce decree, which had been filed in Maryland. Hence our trip to Maryland. So, telling no one, we got into my car and headed out to meet our destiny.

I was pregnant and could not wait for my baby to be

born, for the white picket fence, and for the home filled with love. I was ready to settle down and be a mommy and wife. When Tina was born, I was ecstatic. Brenda joined our family thirteen months later. I loved my babies so much, but Gene did not seem to know what to do with them. Before they were born, he was as excited as any expectant father. He wanted to be there for Tina's birth, but in those days fathers were not allowed into the delivery room. Instead, Gene went out, got drunk, and wound up in a fistfight with our landlord.

He spent the rest of the night sleeping it off in a drunk tank, and I was worried that we would be evicted.

I wondered if he he had been thinking about the daughter he had with his first wife but had never seen.

At least we both loved country music.

TEN
The In-law (1966)

We did not get evicted. After living in a rental apartment with the two girls, we found our dream house. It had five bedrooms, a dining room, a kitchen, a living room with a working fireplace, and a big front porch. There was a detached one-car garage. The biggest selling point for us was that it was only a short walk to my childhood home, where my parents still lived.

Gene insisted that we have enough space so that when my parents aged, we would have enough room for them to live with us. We took out a GI loan, a reward given to veterans, which lowered the interest rates on a mortgage. Things were looking up.

The first night in our new home, guess who got drunk and slept on a mattress in the detached garage? Whenever things looked up, Gene sank down.

He had a good job in the up-and-coming field of computer programming. I was teaching. We had two adorable little girls, two loving grandparents, and the white picket fence. From all appearances we were the perfect family.

Not!

When Gene suggested sending for his father, I saw no reason to deny him the opportunity to reestablish this relationship. I was even a little excited that my children would have the chance to have another grandparent to love them.

Indeed, Herman Allen lived up to my initial expecta-tions—for a minute. He came bearing teddy bears for each of his granddaughters. He showed them the affection that he never allowed himself to shower on his own sons. How-ever, he was not happy that, while Gene was in the army, he had changed the spelling of his last name from Allen to Al-lan. Herman took it personally. Rightfully so. Gene meant it to separate himself from his father.

Our first conversation, over dinner, exposed a man who was prejudiced and ignorant of the ways of the world. He told me that he had never known a Jewish person before meeting me. He seemed proud of that. He also maintained that all New Yorkers were commies. We had ourselves one hell of a redneck living with us.

But he *was* gentle with his grandchildren, despite their Jewish blood.

Gene's mother had died of a self-inflicted abortion while Gene was still a toddler. He did not learn of the reason for his mother's death until he was in his late teens when his uncle divulged the secret. It devastated him and gave him another reason to hate his father—and himself.

Soon after the death of his wife, Herman married Ai-leen. Gene's stepmother was the recipient of violence. She did her best to protect Gene and Philip, Gene's half brother, from this savage being. When she finally broke away from Herman, she wanted to take both boys with her. As the stepmother, she had no legal claim, and so Gene was left in the care of his father.

Herman was certainly no role model. He was a nasty, abusive drunk. Because there was no one else handy, Gene bore the brunt of his abuse.

It should not have been a surprise that, at the age of sixteen, Gene wound up in Chillicothe, a juvenile detention facility. He had been convicted of driving a stolen car over state lines.

While in custody, he met Catherine and Peter Marshall. Peter Marshall was a man of deep faith who lived his faith by, among other things, helping those less fortunate. He found Gene at this most vulnerable point in his life.

This couple took him into their home. When he came of age, they sent him to a Christian college, where he stayed a few months until he was caught defying the no-smoking rule. The Marshalls were good Christian people who believed that Gene was salvageable. They tried, and they cared, but the time was not yet right. Too much damage had been done. However, Gene never forgot the Marshalls' kindness toward him.

Catherine's book, *A Man Called Peter*, was made into a movie.

My heart ached for the boy he was, and I understood how he turned into the man he became.

And so it came to pass that my father-in-law was spared the humiliation of dying in the gutter, only to be murdered in the kitchen by his son. Ironic?

ELEVEN
The Adjudication (1967)

The trial date was set, and we were in the process of picking a jury. George had chosen to add a criminal lawyer to his team. The two of them set out to do the best they could for Gene. I hung out in the corridors of the courthouse. As a potential witness, I was not allowed in to hear the proceedings. I became friendly with the court officers, and they did their best to keep me informed. Still, it was harrowing to be out there, trying to imagine what was going on behind those doors. Family did come out to keep me posted. Again, my mother was my greatest source of strength. She was in the courtroom as often as she was able to leave our children with Terry.

Gene's stepmother came to Long Island from Evansville, Indiana. She had endured so much vitriol at the hands of Herman that she had ambivalent feelings about his death. Her interaction with him had been typical of a domestic violence scenario, as illustrated in this cycle of violence.

First, anger would build up over a real or imagined incident. It could be something as minor as a broken shoelace. This would lead to abuse, physical and/or emotional. It was followed by the calm or "honeymoon" phase, where the abuser begs forgiveness and brings flowers or candy—until the next shoelace breaks or the dog barks too loudly.

With the Allen men, this cycle was fueled by heavy drinking. Many years of this cycle had worn Aileen down. She had divorced her abuser and then reconciled with him a number of times. She finally married someone else. But the damage had been done. Years later she had a breakdown complete with shock treatment and loss of memory. Her husband had to ask me not to contact her because her mental state was too fragile. This was hard because she had been there to support Gene's children and me. Although we had never met before this tragedy brought us together, she came with a warning, a message.

She recognized the risk I was taking if I decided to remain with Gene. She saw my life as a reflection of her own and was frightened for me. Her advice still haunts me: "Barbara, he is too much like his father. If you don't leave him, he will destroy you."

I got it, I really did, but a trial was coming up. There was so much at stake. This was not the time to leave him. Not while he was fighting for his life in a court battle.

I listened, and I stored it away.

For now I was surrounded by family members, who tried to shield me.

My Aunt Henrietta and Cousin Norma came from their respective homes in Florida and Connecticut to provide solace and normalcy. We laughed and pretended it was just a girls' sleepover. I remember all of us going to have our hair done for what we thought would be the beginning of the trial. We laughed and showed off our new hairdos at dinner. I learned later on that this is known as "act as if." Just go through the motions and perhaps the feelings would follow. At the time, feeling numb was the only tolerable emotion.

My father was having just as difficult a time as the rest of us. He thought of Gene as a son, had accepted him into his life, and had tried hard to be a positive role model. They would work together doing repairs and renovations on our homes. They would play poker and, unfortunately, go to the shooting range.

My father was incapable of rationalizing how this tragedy could have happened. Although he was aware that his son-in-law was not the nice Jewish professional he had hoped his daughter would bring home to the family, he did recognize positive traits he saw in Gene.

A kind, gentle person, my father was not lacking in machismo. He was a veteran of World War II, a lieutenant colonel in the New York State Guard, and he carried a licensed handgun. But nowhere within himself could he even vaguely understand how anyone could take another person's life. Nor would he turn his back on the father of his grandchildren. He didn't understand the vile act that Gene perpetrated and he did not know how to fix it, but he was there to honor whatever decision I made.

All of them were present during the beginning of what we thought would be a long trial. The jury was being selected when George, my attorney, found me in the courtroom, where he caught me off guard. I knew they were far from completing the panel. I looked at him with curiosity and apprehension. He told me that they were going to stop the trial. Gene had decided that he wanted to accept a plea. Wow! Although not entirely unexpected, it was another earth-shattering moment.

The original defense was to be "not guilty by reason of diminished capacity." This was no "who done it." He had admitted pulling the trigger. Trial would have been a gamble. He had been indicted on Murder One. Although no person had been executed in New York State since 1963, there were still inmates on death row. New York was ambivalent about its desire to kill people. There *were* grounds to suggest premeditation. He had the time to change his mind as he went from room to room to get the rifle.

Still, rational thought would have concluded that this was not a death penalty case, but one does not revel in rationality when facing a murder trial.

Proceeding to trial promised to generate another wave of publicity. In 1966 patricide was a big news event. Sober Gene wanted to spare all of us the stress and embarrassment of a trial.

Now it made sense to look for the most favorable outcome. The decision was made. He, we really, would do two-and-a-half to seven years to be served in Sing Sing prison (not called a correctional facility in those days). Truth in advertising.

Talk about getting a break.

Sentencing day came, an ending and a beginning.

The judge sent a message to me through my attorney, asking if I had anything I would like to say. This was the precursor of a victim's impact statement. In an ironic way I was looked at as a victim/survivor because it was my father-in-law who had been murdered.

I said, "One day Gene is going to come home. He will return first to me and then to society. Will he get help with his psychiatric problems while in prison?"

My hope and expectation had been that they would send him to a forensic hospital or, preferably, to Pilgrim State Psychiatric Hospital, which was in our community. The judge told my attorney to tell me that I should be assured that Gene was finally going to get the help he needed.

I wondered if the judge really believed this.

It is a fact that all the parts of the criminal justice system are disconnected. The police arrest you and, unless they testify at your trial, their role is complete. The judicial sentences you to the Department of Corrections; despite what anyone thinks or desires, the Department of Corrections is autonomous. It is within their jurisdiction to determine where a person serves his or her sentence. The judge might request a particular type of institution, but it makes no difference. The Department of Corrections does not answer to the judiciary. And then, if the prisoner is released to parole or post-release supervision, the parole system takes over.

And so, Gene was sentenced to hard time at Sing Sing prison. The prison system is filled with people like Gene, who are begging for psychiatric care. Back in the 1970s the trend was toward deinstitutionalization of the mentally ill. The consequences of closing the large psychiatric hospitals were that many displaced patients became homeless and non-compliant, no longer taking their prescribed anti-psychotic drugs. Instead, they turned to illegal drugs or alcohol to mask their pain. The prisons became the dumping ground for the mentally ill and the addicted.

No, judge, this was not the answer to my prayers.

TWELVE
Sing Sing (late 1967–early 1968)

We left the courtroom, Gene to be brought back to the jail to await an available bed at Sing Sing and I to go home to our children, shaking but relieved that we now knew our fate. The plea deal was accepted and Gene was heading to a place where "they" said he would get help.

So now the preparation, emotional as well as practical, began. My next visit to the county jail would be the beginning of the end of the familiar.

Amidst the turmoil of awaiting trial, supporting my family, and visiting Gene, I had tried to maintain a degree of sanity.

The year we spent at the Nassau County jail opened my eyes to the unimaginable. I looked up from my own sorrow and saw the people sharing my space in this visiting arena. I saw mothers crying for their wayward children, wives grieving the demise of their marriages, disappointed fathers, confused siblings. A portion of humanity was veiled in secrecy and shame. I felt a kinship, a responsibility towards these families. Look! I'm here too. We are not alone, though each family, each person, cocooned itself away from each other. Now, I wanted to be noticed, to embrace the only people whose heartbeats melded with mine. We were not invisible to each other.

If I noticed fear or a tear in someone's eyes, I spoke a few words. Walter, our guard in this rabbit hole, would whisper to me that someone was going through an exceptionally difficult time. We became coconspirators.

Gradually, I inched towards others. This was a new role for me, something I only discovered about myself when I was thrown into the topsy-turvy world of criminal injustice.

It started with a smile, a word about the weather and, eventually, some truth sharing.

"I'm afraid of what will happen at the next hearing."

"Did your son get Legal Aid? How do I go about it?"

"What should I tell my children?"

"Should I come up with the bail?"

"My daughter is failing in school, or angry, or withdrawing ..."

"He is being sent upstate."

Oh my God, he is going to the big house! Shades of James Cagney. Our only reality was what we saw in the movies. We were leaving what was familiar and heading towards ... what?

Now it was my turn to face the inevitable and ask the most recurring question, "He is being sent upstate! How will I get to see him?" Amidst the turmoil of awaiting trial, supporting my family, and visiting Gene, I had tried to maintain a degree of sanity, but each shift from the norm was a trauma.

I had been putting money in his commissary account. What would happen to that money? Would it follow him, would they return it to me, or would we lose it? I was questioning Walter when a woman standing next to me said that she was about to ask the same question. Her husband was also going to be sent to Sing Sing. We spontaneously smiled, and both of us felt a sense of relief. Here was someone who *got it*. There was someone else in this universe who was scared just like me. We exchanged phone numbers and, since we lived only a town apart, thought that we might be able to console each other and perhaps even carpool to visits.

It worked! Edna and I stayed in each other's lives for many years. Her husband was a compulsive gambler, and his addiction had caused him to steal from his employer. Bill and Gene followed the same route, from Sing Sing to Green Haven, and both were paroled at the same time.

Bill was another person who had an addiction and was thrust into the criminal-justice system. He needed to wait for his release before eventually seeking help at one of the very few if not the only gambling rehab of its time—in Minnesota. Bill's recovery was slow, with many setbacks, but Edna knew that our friendship would stay solid, through better or worse. This is how it was with each of the prison families I would eventually meet.

Edna brought something special into my life. She worked for a pediatrician, and her doctor became the doctor for my children. It was a relief to be able to talk to a physician who understood that our family was experiencing trauma and greeted us with hugs as well as stethoscopes.

I also got to enter the world of the Playboy bunny. Edna's son had a girlfriend who had started work at the Playboy Club in Manhattan. She needed a room to rent, and I needed extra income. Helping Cindy with her makeup and bunny costume was a joy for the girls and me. We did a lot of giggling. Cindy was a ray of sunshine, and the relationship helped me pay my bills.

Having someone in prison is an unexpected financial burden. The expense of gas and tolls, the money you leave for commissary, the monthly packages, plus in my case the loss of my spouse's income, are devastating.

It took a few weeks but, as scheduled, both Gene and Bill were transported to Sing Sing, a mere two-and-a-half-hour drive from Long Island. Considering the options, we were quite fortunate. Most prisons were up north near the Canadian border. But everyone entering the prison system was processed through this notorious prison overlooking the Hudson River in Ossining, New York. Since most of the prisoners and their families lived downstate, it did make sense to keep the facility nearby. It still surprises me that something actually made sense in this rabbit hole.

My mother and father accompanied us on our first visit. Despite the fact that everyone, even the baddest of the bad, was housed in Sing Sing, children were allowed to visit and the visits were contact visits. Visitors and inmates sat on opposite sides of a table and were actually able to touch each other. I had not been able to touch my husband's hand in more than a year. Brenda and Tina were toddlers now, both enrolled in day care, Tina getting ready to begin kindergarten. They were so excited to finally see their father. My father was their male role model and they loved him, but they were curious about this man they barely remembered. All their little friends had such different lives from theirs. They had two parents. Even in a divorce, Daddy visited or took them out on weekends.

I tried to keep his memory alive and read them pieces of his letters. So many of Gene's letters were filled with how much he loved his daughters, and me, and how sorry he was for that horrible moment that caused this separation.

These visits to Sing Sing were so different from the reality of living day to day with this alcoholic, workaholic father. At home, before this event, it was as if he did not know what to do with these two little people who were so dependent and needy. He sensed that they were the most important things in the world to me—more important than he was. He had no parenting skills and, having seldom been nurtured himself, he had nothing to draw upon. His emotional bank was empty. Again, there was ambivalence. Gene knew how he should respond to his family. He saw it in other people, experienced it in the many books he read and the movies he saw, but it was never in his gut.

He was too bright not to know that there was something missing. Occasionally, he tried. Before the tragedy, he liked to take his daughters to the pond where they would feed the ducks. Sometimes he would allow the gentle side of him to peep through, but those moments were few and far between.

We would go on outings, usually with my parents, and we would have fun and laugh—until one beer led to another. He always preferred drive-in movies, building up the backseat of the car so we could put the girls comfortably and safely in their carriers, all strapped in before seat belts were standard in cars.

Of course, you could easily bring a cooler to a drive-in theater.

In Sing Sing there was no beer. But there were lots of hugs and sitting on Daddy's lap. There were funny things, too. Tina's day-care class designed paperweights made of rocks. They were Father's Day gifts for the daddies.

She wanted to bring hers to her father. It was painted, really pretty, and personalized—"To Daddy, from Tina." Oh, how naïve we were! Can you picture bringing a BIG rock into a prison?

Tina was accepting of the fact that we would have to save it until Daddy came home. Daddy told her to put the rock in his bedroom; when he came home, we would celebrate her creativity over an ice cream sundae.

Tina was always non-confrontational. If she was told she could not do something, she would not outwardly rebel. Brenda? Not so much. She wanted her father to have that rock and was not shy about expressing her feelings. She did not win the battle but, on a positive note, we did not lose visiting privileges.

Once a week while their father was in Sing Sing, my girls had a loving and sober father. We were allowed in to visit, but there were always barriers in the way. I could not bring in essentials for the children, such as snacks, pacifiers, or sippy cups. There were no vending machines; those were to come much later.

At the first visit, all adults were fingerprinted; at each visit thereafter, they took a thumbprint. I guess that was to make sure no one was breaking in.

In state facilities, as opposed to county, we were allowed to bring the inmates packages of food weighing up to thirty-five pounds. After finding a parking spot at the prison, we had a steep hill to navigate. Lugging the packages, with two toddlers hanging on to each other and gun towers looming over us, was quite an undertaking. If we strayed from the path, a booming voice echoed from those towers to set us right.

As usual, my parents were my rock. We all traveled up for the first visit, not having any idea what to expect, our minds flashing back to old prison movies. We got through the preliminary processing. After the initial visit, my mother was informed she would no longer be allowed visiting privileges; married women were restricted from visiting unless accompanied by certain categories of men. A sister-in-law could visit if the felon's brother was with her. Apparently this directive was sent out by a man who listened to mother-in-law jokes or had a bad relationship with his own wife's mother.

Believe me, my mother did not enjoy those trips to hell, but she wanted to be there to support me.

How dare they be so presumptive and sexist!

I wrote letters, made many phone calls, and was eventually told that my mother would be allowed to visit. They were going to make an exception for my mother. It was not exactly like winning the lottery, but my social conscience was now aroused, and I would not stop advocating until they did rescind that ridiculous rule for everyone's mother.

I'm not sure how many people appreciated that, but it was just wrong.

Oh, I was learning.

Another time, I traveled up with a wife I had met on a prior visit. She also lived on Long Island, and we were able to travel together a few times, taking turns driving. One snowy winter day when it was Mary's turn to drive, we arrived at Sing Sing and began the processing procedure. Mary learned that her husband had been transferred to Green Haven, a little over an hour away. She immediately went into panic mode, got into her car, and did not look back—leaving Tina, Brenda, and me without enough money to get home. We needed to take a cab to the train station in Ossining. A cab ride was the only option, since there was no public transportation from the prison to the train station. My route would have been a cab, a train into New York City, and then the Long Island Railroad to Hempstead and finally a bus ride to the corner near my house—very costly and time-consuming. Mind you, Sing Sing was the closest prison to the New York metropolitan area, which consisted of the boroughs that housed the largest percentage of potential offenders.

I did have enough money to call my father, who came to our rescue. As we waited two hours for Dad to arrive from Long Island, I wondered: "Why am I doing this?"

The children did have the opportunity to bond with their father. It was a sober time and a time of reflection for

Gene. He showed his daughters a side of him that had not been visible during the tumult of daily living and drinking. And therefore, although it was not easy, I continued doing this.

THIRTEEN
The Fortune Society (1968)

It was a Sunday night. The girls were sleeping, the chores were done, and my lesson plans were prepared for the next day. My daily letter to Gene was written and ready for the mailbox. I knew that he had nothing to look forward to but the mail he received from me. I was his touchstone to the outside world. I took a "me break" to have a cup of coffee and scan the newspaper. A caption caught my eye instantly. The David Susskind Show was going to host a panel of ex-cons disseminating information about the New York State prison system. It would air at 11:00 P.M., late for a school night.

Getting the girls bathed, reading a bedtime story, cleaning up after dinner, and getting my lesson plans written for the upcoming school week left me little time to write to Gene. I was physically and emotionally drained by then. All I craved was bedtime, my chance to decompress, to escape the constant undercurrent of fear and anxiety that I endured every waking moment.

But I was drawn to the TV and at 11:00 that Sunday night I made myself comfortable in the living room and turned on the David Susskind show, a decision that was to impact the rest of my life. I was mesmerized by this panel of four ex-cons talking about how they barely survived their stays as guests of the New York State penal system. I was alarmed and listened in awe as they described the conditions of confinement.

These strangers inside my TV and now inside my head brought me into the loneliness of living in a barred cage, surrounded by the noises of so many grown men moaning and crying in their sleep, screaming and calling for their mothers. It was difficult to hear this as I imagined Gene lying in his cell listening to this symphony of sounds, perhaps contributing to the melody. And me not being there to comfort him.

I still did not sleep in our bed. I could not bear to reach out and feel the empty space. I wonder what I missed. It was strange that in his absence I remembered only the gentleness and loving gestures. I empathized with what I imagined was his despair. Lying alone on his cot, remembering as I did, and feeling the loneliness, though he was not alone, surrounded by unwanted sounds and smells. He had no way to escape the senses.

I was left with the images of savage beatings by officers and tier mates, the yard as a battlefield, the avoidance of someone approaching you, not being sure if you were in danger. I reminded myself to ask him on our next visit: "Has anyone tried to rape you?"

As the Susskind program progressed and these four men spoke of the dehumanizing and degrading incidents that occurred day after day in this taxpayer-funded hell, I became enraged. My mind drifted back to my visit to Rikers Island. As a student at Hofstra College, I had taken a criminal-justice course. As part of the curriculum, we were required to tour this notorious New York City jail. I had looked around the facility and was filled with horror; the sights appalled me. It was the twentieth century, and they still locked people away in cages. I had no clue then that I would one day be caught up in this quagmire.

The panelists gave an address in New York City for their newly formed organization, which they were calling the Fortune Society, befitting an organization of thieves, stolen from a play, *Fortune in Men's Eyes*. David Rothenberg had produced this play, written by and about John Herbert, who was brutalized in a Canadian prison.

Of course, I could not sleep that night. My mind was filled with visions of the imagined horrors inflicted on Gene.

The next day I wrote a letter to the Fortune Society and said I wanted to find a way to become part of this movement, but I lived thirty miles away, was a single mother with two small children, and was a school teacher. I told "To Whom It May Concern" that my husband was in prison, and I was doing my time on the outside.

I did get a response to my letter, from someone named David Rothenberg. The very same.

He invited me to a meeting at the Actor's Playhouse on Sheridan Square in Greenwich Village, the theater where the play originated. He asked, "If you are not able to be there, do I have permission to read your letter?"

Of course I was going to be there! That is, if my father would go with me. I was not prepared to be in the company of thieves and worse without the company of a person with a gun ... and a permit to carry it. My father and I took the forty-five minute drive to downtown Manhattan, leaving my mother at home with my daughters, where I am sure she suffered a torturous few hours imagining the fate that awaited us and regretting that she did not chain the front door shut to prevent us from leaving.

Dad and I reached our destination. I was trembling, and he kept assuring me that we could turn back. Of course, we continued into this off-Broadway theater and looked around, not knowing what to expect.

There we met the cast of characters.

There was tall, redheaded, gangly Kenny Jackson, with his wife, the beautiful Lorraine. They were to become my friends, my family, and my protectors. It was Kenny who saved my life and my sanity and with whom I was to develop a special bond that lasted until the day he died.

The walls of Coxsackie—or as he called it, the "bucket of blood"—could not contain the passion in Kenny's soul. They might have knocked his teeth out and kept him locked away in solitary confinement, but he rose from the depths of hell and made criminal-justice history.

Kenny discovered and joined Alcoholics Anonymous and became an evangelist for sobriety. Everyone he met there became his "pigeon." As a result of watching the David Susskind show, Kenny appeared at David Rothenberg's office doorstep and became the first Fortune counselor. In his own inimitable and unorthodox way, Kenny went on a mission to change the criminal-justice system and all those affected by it.

While changing the world, Kenny had a deep effect on my life. If I had no one to accompany me on the drive to Sing Sing or Green Haven, Kenny would go with me while Lorraine stayed with Tina and Brenda.

During these journeys, we spoke about alcoholism. Kenny convinced me that Gene was an alcoholic, using booze as his drug of choice to mask the pain of his "mental illness." I always admitted that Gene had some sort of psychosis, but I knew nothing about alcoholism. My image of an alcoholic was of someone sleeping in a cardboard box, in a doorway, in the Bowery. Gene left for work each day in a three-piece suit and functioned quite normally, except when he had those "episodes." It was easier for me to accept him having a psychiatric illness than being a drunk.

This was my introduction to alcoholism, Al-Anon, and the beginning of my healing. The knowledge I gained there gave me the tools to begin my journey to practice the twelve steps of recovery. Though I was not an alcoholic, Gene's disease affected me and everyone in our family circle. Something had to change and because I could not change Gene, I had to revisit my reaction to his behavior. This was a lesson that I carried with me throughout all future encounters and a mantra I used in all the groups I later facilitated.

Years down the road Kenny would be there to physically protect me during Gene's episodes of violence following his release from prison. Kenny drove from Bedford Stuyvesant in the middle of the night when I hysterically called him to tell him that Gene had driven my little Metropolitan into the front stoop of my parents' home, where

I had fled to escape his latest episode of aggression.

Kenny was the first one I called after Gene burned my house down.

In this theater I also met Marjorie O'Keefe. Marjorie, with her long legs, dark black hair, and slender body, showed up at Fortune because she had a boyfriend on Rikers Island. Marjorie and I clicked as friends immediately upon meeting that night in Greenwich Village. Eventually, we were both asked to serve on the newly formed Board of Directors of the Fortune Society.

We spent days sitting on my front porch while Marjorie strummed country music on her guitar. We cried and laughed, drinking wine or apricot sours while trying to make sense of our lives. I am not sure we ever did.

Lorraine, affectionately called Larry, usually joined us. When Lorraine and Kenny met, he did not have a driver's license. She served as chauffeur, not only to Kenny but to many of the newly released men and occasional woman as they traveled to speaking engagements, meetings, and twelve-step calls. Kenny and Lorraine were known as Uncle Kenny and Aunt Larry to Tina and Brenda. Lorraine's two children, Debbie and Donald, were slightly older than my girls, but they all bonded.

I miss Marge. I am not sure how we lost touch but we did. I hope she found serenity. Larry and I still keep in touch. She and Kenny married and had a daughter, Jen.

Kenny died of a heart attack at fifty-five years old.

Larry lost both Kenny and Donald but is now a grandmother and great-grandmother.

Of course, there was David Rothenberg, without whom none of this could be possible.

My house in Hempstead was a safe haven for a group of people who were learning to adapt to an unaccepting world. It became a sanctuary for my Fortune family. Most lived in depressed areas of the city; here in suburbia we could have cookouts with our children in the back yard, play stickball in the street, and sit on the front porch, breathing in the clean air.

Kenny was quick to inform me that here was the perfect place to bring folks who were transitioning from prison because they could eat my food as a bridge from lockdown prison chow to Mama's home cooking.

Mel Rivers showed up at Fortune shortly after getting out of prison. He came to case the place and, surprise, he found a partner—a speaking partner, not a crime partner. He and Kenny, who together became known as Salt and Pepper, went out to inform the world that taxpayers were paying a hefty price to support a failing penal system. They spoke to anyone who would listen—in basements of churches, schools, colleges, civic groups, and on radio and TV.

Mel is now living the straight life in Arizona, happily married. He occasionally returns to his roots and visits Fortune. He returns as a role model, a success in a system used to failures.

As Tina, Brenda, and I watched one of Kenny and Mel's TV appearances, Brenda was shocked to learn that Uncle Kenny had been in jail. Tina immediately put her mind at ease by saying that Uncle Kenny "accidentally robbed someone."

Whenever I was able, I went with Kenny and Mel and spoke about the effects of incarceration on families.

Eddie Morris was brought to Fortune by Isadore Zimmerman. Izzy and Eddie did time together upstate. Izzy was wrongfully convicted of a murder and released from death row right before his execution. His book, *Punishment without Crime,* should have been a template against the death penalty and wrongful convictions.

Izzy became the first president of the Fortune Society and won a million dollars in compensation from the State of New York. Unfortunately, he died four months later and did not have the satisfaction of spending the money.

Eddie was in and out of youth facilities and prisons almost all his life. A sensitive, bright man, he had difficulty relating to straight people. He spent a lot of time at 10 Foster Place. Here he practiced the art of seduction. Many a visitor to our "three-quarter-way" house succumbed to Eddie's charm. During the time he was hanging out with us, he was really trying to live an honest life, speaking and working with Fortune.

It was not to last forever. Eventually Eddie returned to a life of crime and got shot while trying to hold up an illegal gambling event. To my knowledge he never did go back to robbing regular citizens. Eddie returned to prison from the hospital where they treated his wounds, but no one could treat his psyche. The last I heard from him, he was in Bellevue Hospital's homeless shelter, angry and in the throes of addiction. He begged to come and live with me. With a heavy heart, I refused. I never heard from him again.

Pat McGarry's voice resonated after a performance of *Fortune and Men's Eyes*, explaining that the times he spent in New York State prisons were tougher than those depicted in the play. That is what led to the Tuesday discussions after the performances and eventually to the David Susskind show. Pat, an openly gay man at a time when it was not common to flaunt one's sexuality, loved playing stickball outside my house

Charles McGregor was another person who came to Fortune after years in prison. He was also on the speaking circuit. Watching this big, bald black man playing stickball with skinny, purse-carrying Pat McGarry was amazing. Charles eventually made it to Hollywood and can still be seen on late night TV in *Blazing Saddles* or *Super Fly*. Little did we realize that we were nurturing a future movie actor. After many years in prison, Charles turned his life around and brought laughter to his film audience. He passed away in 1996.

Charlie was not the only the only Fortune alum to transition to Hollywood. Chuck Bergansky, another long termer, also followed the path to glamour and success.

I found myself in the company of celebrities I would never have met but for David Rothenberg. David would take me to previews or opening nights at the theater, where I would go backstage with him and be introduced to the stars of Broadway productions.

We never knew whom we would meet at Fortune

events. Many celebrities were supporters of Fortune, and they would graciously lend their names and give their time to help raise money or awareness.

It was at a Fortune fundraiser that I met the star of M*A*S*H, Mike Farrell. Of course, I was flustered and star struck, but that gave way to awe when I realized that he would be accompanying us to Long Island. David was scheduled to debate Dennis Dillon, the long-time District Attorney of Nassau County, on the death penalty. Mike (we were now on a first name basis) decided to tag along. That was how I wound up sitting in the backseat for the almost hour ride from Manhattan to Garden City, with the handsome, talented Mike Farrell. How important I felt when we walked into that gathering together.

I saw Mike a few times after that. The last time was about a year ago when he, David, and I took the subway. We were leaving The Castle, where Mike surprised the residents by showing up for a Thursday night house meeting.

For me these were the best of times and the worst of times.

FOURTEEN
Prison Families Anonymous (1974)

Amid all the chaos in my private life, our list of families grew. Each call from a new family confirmed the need for a support group like Prison Families Anonymous. We were the hidden victims and little thought was given to us. We were collateral damage. No one in the system thought to include us in decision-making or cared to share information with us. What little information there was started with an attorney. It wasn't much. Although the family left behind was usually the person paying, we were politely told to mind our own business. Lawyer-client privilege and all that.

From there it got worse.

The criminal-justice system is impossible to navigate. Even the language is intimidating. What is the difference between a misdemeanor and a felony? What is an arraignment, an indictment, a plea deal, a probation report? What is the difference between a jail and a prison? What is a commissary?

There was a whole new vocabulary to learn.

Where will they take my husband, and can I see him? How do I deal with the shame? What do I tell my children? Will they be bullied in school? How do I pay for all of this? Why am I so angry? Am I overreacting, or are my feelings normal? How *should* I feel?

We had to figure things out on our own. We learned there are no right or wrong feelings. There are no shoulds or musts. We cannot tell you what to do or how to feel, but we can share our experiences, strength, and hope. In time, we realized we could no longer do this sitting around a kitchen table. It was time to grow.

At this point, we were an informal group of families staying in touch with each other. Many folks I met in the visiting room, some Gene sent my way, and still more David Rothenberg sent to me. As the Fortune Society grew and more people called David's PR office, my phone number was widely circulated. Everybody who called said that they did not know that others were experiencing the same pain, confusion, and doubts. As a group, we found that sharing our experiences accelerated our healing. It was a relief to know that we were not going into the rabbit hole by ourselves.

Even with our family members in prison, it was sometimes hard to keep a conversation going. A lot of things were left unsaid. There were many questions I myself was afraid to ask because I was not sure if I could handle the answers. There were long periods of silence. During one of those lapses in communication with my husband, Gene casually asked me if I could see an older couple, a few phones away. I cautiously looked to my left and for the first time, I saw Mickey and Pan Holder. They looked to be in their sixties, both slight in build. Even from this vantage point, I noticed the anguish on their faces and saw that the hand holding the phone receiver was trembling.

Gene told me the tale of Howard Holder, their son, the man behind their area of the Plexiglas. Howard was the principal of a school in Brooklyn and a member of the Valley Stream school board. He and his paramour, Lenore, a teacher and colleague, were accused and eventually convicted of conspiracy in the murder of Howard's wife, Joan.

They had been asleep in their marital bed when *someone* sneaked into the bedroom, giving Joan enough chloroform to cause her death and Howard just enough to cause him to lose consciousness.

Howard left his three vulnerable teenage youngsters in the care of his parents, who moved from their home in Brooklyn into the house Howard had shared with his family. The grandparents did not want to uproot the children. This way they could remain in their schools and not be traumatized any more than was unavoidable. The death of a parent is always traumatic, but to have your mother murdered in her bed and your father accused of the crime is horrendous beyond understanding. So, while going through their own grief, Mickey and Pan stepped in to care for the children.

I kept sneaking glances at this elderly, frail couple. Gene told me, "Howard is worried about his father. He is taking some kind of meds to help him cope, but he really is falling apart. Do you think you could talk to them, Barbara?"

As we left the visiting area, I hesitantly approached them. "Hi. Are you okay? It is so hard coming here, isn't it?" I could see tears welling in his eyes so I put my hand on Pan's arm.

He smiled and softly said, "Thank you."

I felt an unexpected kinship with this unknown couple. Except that I did know them. We were bonded by a force inhaled but not yet recognized. After leaving the jail, we stopped for the first of many cups of tea. I was blessed to have met them. At the time I had no idea of the impact they would have on my life.

We coordinated the times of our visits. It was comforting to see a familiar person in the visiting room and to know that we would have some time together after the visit to decompress. We weren't so lonely afterward. Although we still had the same fears and desperation, some of the edge was taken away.

Practically nothing else had changed. We were still crowded into that visiting area, speaking loudly so that our voices might rise above the others, trying to hear and be heard through those telephone lines. At five-feet-three inches, I had to stand on tippy-toes just to see my husband. For their part, the Holders were still trying to hold on for dear life; we clung to each other for support.

It was easy to be enamored with the Holders. Pan was a true gentleman. As a young couple, they spent vacations in the Catskill Mountains. Pan would entertain the others by playing his flute. He had derived his nickname from the mythical flute-playing Greek god who was said to roam the mountains during ancient times.

Mickey had to draw upon all her strength to continue to nurture her family and to allow herself to believe in Howard's innocence. She questioned her loyalty to a son, who she thought might be a murderer. I understood. I questioned my loyalty to my husband, who I knew *was* a murderer.

Eventually, Howard and Lenore were sentenced and sent upstate. Though we were no longer going to the jail, we continued spending time together; they became my extended family.

After a few years, Howard and Lenore were released from prison. They got married and moved back to the scene of the crime. The elder Holders moved to Ohio where another son welcomed them. The children grew up, went out on their own, and are leading successful lives.

***

Years later, after Prison Families Anonymous formed, Sally and Al came to our Hempstead meeting. Their son was in a jail in California. Al had called the Fortune Society looking for direction and was given our telephone number. They, like the Holders, were the gentlest of people and lived lives as far removed from jails and prisons as you can get. These families were the collateral damage.

Sally was our brownie lady. She baked her brownies with love and always brought enough so that we could bring some home to our children. My girls did resent that Mommy went out every single Friday night, but the brownies sweetened the pot somewhat. Al, a CPA, served on our board of directors.

Through these wonderful people, I discovered a me I did not know existed. Until I was thrown into this topsy-turvy world of criminal injustice, I was always the kid picked last for the team, the girl at the end of the line, too timid to object to those pushing ahead of me. My very first job as an usher in a local movie house lasted one night because I was "too shy." I was the child who stood the straightest in line as the teacher walked us down the corridor in elementary school.

"Don't pursue the dream of majoring in journalism," my mother had advised. "So, what will you do? Teach English in high school?"

No! I did switch my major, but I became an elementary-school teacher, as befitted a girl raised in the '40s and '50s. Never rock the boat. Don't call attention to yourself. I was voiceless.

But I did find a voice because my voice was needed so that I could stand tall with and for these awesome people.

The prison families I have met on this journey are some of the strongest, most amazing people I know. It started with Edna, Pan, and Mickey at county, and it continues to this day through the people who continue to call PFA. Each new encounter causes me to realize that I am surrounded by energy, spirit, and vitality. Even laughter!

FIFTEEN
Gallows Humor (Over the years)

There is wrenching pain, of course, but there is humor where least expected and when most needed. It is gallows humor, perhaps, but sometimes we do have to laugh at some of the bizarre situations we get ourselves into.

Since both of their sons were in the same upstate prison, Jackie and Camille decided to car pool for their four-hour ride to the northern country. The trip was planned for weeks. They would split the driving and the cost of gas and tolls. Everything was thought out, except which route they would take. It turned out that it was the blind leading the blind. Neither had a GPS, and each depended on the other for directions. After spending an entire day driving through the mountains and valleys of upstate New York, with a detour through New Jersey, they never did find the prison. They returned to Long Island exhausted and disappointed, without seeing their sons.

That could have been a semi-tragedy, but because they were on this journey together, they were able to see the absurdity of their situation; rather than moan and groan, when they told their tale of woe at our next meeting, there was hysterical laughter.

When we needed a good laugh we could always depend on Rae, whose grandson had been arrested as a teenager and charged with a gang-related crime. Rae swore her grandson was innocent. Depending upon the season, she wore a sweatshirt or a tee shirt with his picture and the word *Innocent* emblazoned on the front. She never left home without it; she wore it to the market, to the doctor's office, to speaking engagements, to meetings with representatives, and to prison visits. Rae had a braid reaching down toward her ankles, and she pledged not to cut her hair until Reed came home.

Rae visited Reed as often as she could get a ride; when she did, she carried a well-stocked package of goodies. She was determined that he would enjoy what she chose to put in that box. Food packages were sent with a part of our hearts wrapped inside.

Not only do we put a lot of thought into what we will include in these care packages, we invest a lot of money. Rae bought a block of expensive cheese she knew that her grandson would enjoy. She handed the heavy box with all the goodies, including the cheese, to the correction officer on package duty. She went into the visiting room to enjoy the time spent with Reed. When she was checking out, the officer advised Rae that everything could get in except the block of cheese. She grudgingly took the cheese home.

She wasn't about to give up. She and Reed both did their research and found there was nothing in the rules and regulations that said cheese had to be sliced. She brought that same block back the next time she visited. Again it was refused. Rae determined to win the battle. That cheese block travelled back and forth with her until, after weeks of refusal, some officer let that cheese get through. The battle was over.

Meeting after meeting, Rae kept us up to date on the saga of the cheese. Each time she told the story, it got funnier and funnier until the laughter became uncontrollable.

Rae did live to see Reed come home but not long enough to cut her braid. She left us on December 28, 2016.

***

The first time I saw Joan C., she was sitting in her car, saying her rosary while waiting for the meeting to start. I was anxious to greet her, thinking that she would probably be a little shy, perhaps praying for the strength to come into a room filled with strangers. Wrong! I met a woman who was strong as a rock, with a vocabulary to make a sailor blush and the capacity to always make us laugh when she would tell it exactly as it is. As self-determined as she is, Joan has a heart of gold and will do anything for anyone.

Her son was given a very long sentence. After he had been turned down for parole twice, Joan decided to be more proactive. We found out that Andrea Evans, the chairperson of the Parole Board, was going to be at an event in New York City. Joan convinced me to drive over the bridge and into the city to track Ms. Evans down. Letters and phone calls didn't work, so she needed to plead, woman to woman, face to face.

We did catch up with the commissioner as she was walking out the door of the venue where the event was held. Joan approached her and insisted on having "a few words about my son." Joan had her say, and Commissioner

Andrea Evans was trapped into listening. To her credit, she was polite and kind to Joan. However, it didn't do a bit of good. Five years and two parole hearings later, Joan's son is still behind bars. But the story of the night we stalked a parole commissioner led to some funny moments in the retelling.

When newcomers walk into a room of smiling, laughing people, they think they are in the wrong place. I always promise each of them that one day they will also be laughing.

SIXTEEN
Crying Time (Over the years)

We also have had our share of tragedies. The biggest fear that many of our parents face is one of longevity. "What will happen if I die before he comes home? Who will be there to help him, and where will he go?" It is of real concern when your child is sentenced to a twenty-year prison term.

Dottie did not live to see Michael come home. In New York State, if a close relative (parent, guardian, spouse, sibling, grandparent, child, or grandchild) is near death, the prisoner has a choice of being allowed a deathbed visit or attendance at the funeral. They cannot do both. Mike chose to see his mother before she passed.

I don't much care for the alternative. I've been a witness to shackled prisoners at funeral homes too many times. Depending on the whim of the escorting officers, the grieving person might have his restraints removed and be allowed to sit with the family to mourn, surrounded by loved ones. On the other hand, I recently attended a funeral where a grieving son was kept in a side room, with only his guard for company, while his family was in the adjoining room viewing the deceased. He could actually hear the cries of his father and siblings, but he was helpless. After everyone was asked to leave, his keepers escorted him to the casket, where he was able to get a last glimpse of his mother. There was no one next to him but an uncaring officer, no one to offer him comfort.

I define that as cruel and unusual punishment.

Whatever the choice of homecoming, before or after death, an inmate has to return to the facility to grieve alone. Sometimes, there is someone with compassion back in the cell block. Warren was there for Michael. Warren suffered the same pain when Gerry, his mom, died. He was willing to share his own feelings and help Michael through the grieving process.

Both of their mothers were a part of our prison families, although many years apart.

We have attended far too many funerals of our children. Drugs and incarceration go hand in hand and drugs kill. The first PFA death I recall was the son of Ruth and Richard. He had stolen money and valuables and threatened to cause them bodily harm when they did confront him. As the addiction progressed, he became physically abusive. They put him out of the house, going so far as to change the locks on the door. One night they were in so much fear that that they asked Gene and me to stay with them overnight. Days later, his body was found in the woods near the house, a needle still stuck in his arm.

They never stopped blaming themselves. "If only we had not thrown him out …" We understood. You are damned if you do and you are damned if you don't.

This was in the early 1980s, before the opioid epidemic became so wide spread. Now Narcan, a nasal spray used in overdose situations, has saved some lives.

Todd was brought back from near death time after time. He was arrested for possession and was left to detox in jail. If his mother didn't bail him out, he'd sit there for a while, with no real treatment, until he was released to start the cycle over again. If he gets bailed out again, as we have witnessed time after time, he probably will go back to using. The next time, the overdose may kill him.

What's a mother to do? We know that we are powerless.

We have lost beloved members of our group, some much too young. I cannot help but wonder if the stress the families feel exacerbates their physical ailments. The names are too many, but as with any family, they stay with us in our hearts. They are missed and remembered.

SEVENTEEN
Putting the Pieces Together (the 1970s)

Karen Martin, our cofounder, had a vision for Prison Families Anonymous. If we were going to grow and become a viable force in the criminal-justice community, we needed to incorporate and change our structure. It was time to establish bylaws, a mission statement, and seek funding.

Our first governing body was called a Group Council, with only our families directing us. I was perfectly satisfied with things as they were. I did not want to get caught up in politics and have to account to government funding sources. I thought it would be impossible to advocate for our population and not oppose governmental agencies.

More practical heads prevailed, and we applied for nonprofit status, which restricted our fundraising to private foundations.

One of our initial steps was to approach David Kadane, a law professor at Hofstra University, my alma mater. David was the first director of Hofstra's Neighborhood Law Office, established to serve low-income families. Who better to assist our grassroots organization? David, with the assistance of Jonathan Gradess, now the executive director of the New York State Defenders Association, helped with our incorporation and stayed on to serve as a member of our advisory board.

Our mission statement read: "Prison Families Anonymous, Inc. is a support group for families who have a loved one involved in the criminal or juvenile justice system. Through this support, families and friends learn to cope with the incarceration and the transition of family reunification."

We received our seed money from the Veatch Foundation of the Unitarian Universalist Congregation. That money, a grant from United Way, and some private donations enabled us to move forward. We opened an office and hired an excellent staff. Karen was executive director. Eventually, Dee Cunningham, my Al-Anon sponsor, a mother of four, and the wife of someone who was in and out of jail, became our project director. Maddie Copolla was hired as our secretary. In title she was a secretary, but in reality she was the backbone of our agency.

We hired Trudy Kuntz and Joan Spranger as outreach workers. I met Trudy shortly after her son escaped from the work-release facility at the Nassau County Jail. He left Trudy and her husband to face the possible loss of a considerable amount of bail money. Trudy reached out to Kenny Jackson for advice. He was then running the Offender Rehabilitation and Treatment (ORT) program at Rikers Island, where Trudy was doing some volunteer work. Kenny told Trudy, "You have to call Barbara Allan."

At one point Trudy was contacted by a priest who told her that her son might be in Montreal, Canada. She persuaded Cathy Gibalaro and me to go with her on a mission to find and save her boy. She just wanted to see that he was safe and maybe persuade him to come home and go for help. Perhaps she wanted to be reassured that he was still alive. The three of us, not experienced bounty hunters, drove across our northern border and searched all the places where we thought we might find a homeless, addicted American fugitive. He was not in any of the flop houses, sanctuary houses, or bars we looked in. We returned home.

After years of concern, litigation, and very limited contact with her son, Trudy was able to have the bail money returned to her.

Trudy died very recently, never having learned the fate of her son.

Joan Spranger was dealing with an alcoholic husband when fate or coincidence brought Dee into her life. We knew that Joan needed a job and that she would fit in very nicely with our dysfunctional group.

With this staff, volunteers, and input from our board of directors, we were able to do advocacy work and better serve our families. We sent outreach workers into the courts and both of the Long Island jails. We became members of criminal-justice task forces and worked with many alphabet agencies, such as TASC, EAC, LICA, and we moved our weekly family support meetings out of our houses and into public spaces.

We needed a logo that we could use on our stationery and other written materials, something that was easily recognizable. Karen, executive director and our in-house artist, designed a logo that went right to the heart of who we were. What could define a prison family better than a heart behind bars? It was made into a necklace in 1979, and I wear it on a chain around my neck every time I represent PFA. It is my most precious possession.

We kept a file of every prison in New York State, with information about visiting procedures, contact information for chaplains, counselors, watch commanders, and medical personnel. We provided lists of commissary items and their prices. We had a file with directions to each of the NYS prisons. As a family called for information, we needed to know that we had the answers at our fingertips. The task was overwhelming because each prison was autonomous. It was far from one-size-fits-all, and the rules could change as we were printing them out. I suppose we were the Google of the 1970s.

We started a couples group because Debbie's husband was recently assigned to work-release, a program where a person who is nearing the end of his sentence is allowed to work during the day and return to a local facility at night. Herb was assigned to the work release facility that existed on the grounds of the Nassau County Jail. He would soon be allowed to spend some nights staying at home with his family. Gradual reunification of a person back to family and community was the goal. Debbie was concerned about Herb's returning to her family. She was not sure that she could trust her husband. She had not gotten over the feeling of betrayal. The man she married and thought she knew had committed serious crimes right under her nose, and she was completely unaware.

Her therapist told her she really needed to learn to trust him.

We understood. Trust had to be rebuilt. The old tapes were still playing in her head, and so far she had no reason to think they might have been replaced.

We approached the administration at the Nassau County Jail, and they agreed that we could bring the wives of the men in the work-release program into the facility and allow the couples to form "couples group."

There was no professional leader. We all sat in a circle; the men and women honestly and openly spoke about their fears and expectations. Together they established coping mechanisms and strategies to deal with the real situations they might encounter. When the first man was released, the remaining members of the group were allowed to leave the facility one night a week to continue the sessions in our office.

Of that original couples group, to the best of my knowledge, there was one divorce and no re-arrests.

There is a life lesson that came from this group. One of the couples and their two children traveled upstate for a vacation. Their eleven-year-old son was watching the scenery from the car window and excitedly uttered, "This was the same road we took to visit Daddy in prison!" Mom and Dad were astounded. They had always told the children that they were visiting Daddy at the school where he worked. All that time they thought they had their kids fooled!

We started a children's group because our young ones asked for it. My daughters Tina and Brenda, Dee's daughter Lisa, and some of the other children were in my house, hanging out together while we parents were holding a meeting. As things were winding down, our children handed us a note saying that they wanted to have a group like the grownups.

We hired Shelly Shulman, a dear friend and therapist, who at that time, was running a program for "at risk" youth at Hofstra University. He was the perfect role model for these young people who had lost trust in and felt abandoned by their own fathers. Shelly was compassionate, dependable, and accessible. He was the antithesis of what most of these children had experienced in their primary families.

The kids had a great time, not only meeting regularly but going on dream trips. They visited the Amish Country, the circus, and went to sporting events. They shared popcorn at local cinemas, and they were learning to trust. Life-long friendships were forged.

It was terribly shocking to learn, much later, that Shelly had a history of deprivation in his own past. Shelly was one of four boys. He was the only one to enter into adulthood unscathed. His younger brother, Robert, died in prison after being released from death row into general population. New York had just abolished the death penalty and was no longer in the business of killing people. The cause of Robert's death was listed as natural causes.

When Tina turned seventeen, she worked with Norma, who was then the facilitator of the group. Norma had an important influence on Tina, who was going through some life challenges. She was a mentor, confidant, and role model for all the children, but she and Tina developed a special bond, Unfortunately, Norma died of cancer while still in her prime. We never hired anyone to replace her.

We work with people coming home from prison because our families are being reunited and the returning citizens are also our families.

We organized criminal-justice conferences here on Long Island. I am proud to say that we had the trust and respect of systems people. Sometimes we disagreed, but they would speak to our families at membership meetings or present at our conferences.

Once a month we held open meetings, and we invited people to come and speak to us. We hosted representatives from parole, probation, the Department of Correctional Services, and nonprofit agencies. Anyone who could offer our families knowledge or hope was invited. We never had a problem getting a speaker.

Professionals began reaching out to us, asking if they could offer their expertise. One day in 1976, we got a telephone call from a gentleman who told Maddie that he was a motivational speaker who had just published a book. He wondered if he could offer his expertise to us. The man's name was Wayne Dyer; the book he was referring to was, *Your Erroneous Zone,* the first of many books he would have published.

What a privilege and honor it was for us to welcome Wayne Dyer to a meeting in a basement meeting hall in a church in Hempstead.

We started hearing from people in other states asking how to start a prison family program. It was back in 1973 when a reporter from an Akron, Ohio, newspaper phoned to ask about support for a reader who contacted his paper. As a good reporter should, he investigated and found us.

Karen, Dee, and I drove all night to meet the reporter at the paper. We didn't have the money for a hotel room, so we had the meeting, did a radio interview, and drove right home again. I remember the year because, while we were in the newsroom, the ticker tape came through with the news that Roe vs. Wade was decided.

With the assistance of the *Akron Tribune*, we now had our first auxiliary group.

My next venture to expand the scope of PFA was a trip to Dallas, Texas. At the request of his counterpart in Dallas, Brother Jack Moylan, the director of the Office of Prison Ministry of the Diocese of Rockville Centre (Long Island), sponsored a trip to Dallas to help start a PFA group there. He arranged for me to stay at a convent and to have my expenses paid.

I have one vivid memory of that trip. The sisters held a meeting with some prison families in their parish. And for the first time I met a woman who had a son on death row. Unfortunately, that was not the last encounter of this kind.

We helped start groups all over the country. Dee drove to Connecticut a few times to assist a local Hartford group start a family support network. We realized we did not have the person power or the money to travel, so we put together a new group packet, with suggestions on how to help families. Groups sprang up in Florida, North Carolina, some upstate New York communities, and even Canada. Without the resources, we could not monitor the many groups. Some called themselves Prison Families Anonymous, but others changed their names and veered from our example. We can only hope that our philosophy of families helping families guided them.

I was invited to appear on a number of talk shows. Some hosts were sensitive and focused on issues. Others were more interested in sensationalizing "the crime." Brenda and I did two segments on *Live with Regis and Kathy Lee*. Kathy was particularly supportive and made us feel as comfortable as one could feel talking about the pain of a loved one's incarceration. When the discussion centered on painful recollections, I felt her squeeze my hand.

Dee and I did a three-state, three-day blitz of shows for Fox News. We flew to Pittsburgh, Baltimore, and I think it was Boston, We were in a haze, with little sleep, but we were determined. It was awkward, especially for me. One of the hosts was very interested in the size of the rifle and the amount of blood spilled. I still cringe at that interview because it seemed as though every time I turned on the TV, that show was in reruns.

But more often we were met with respect, and, most important, we were bringing prison families out of the closet. Families were speaking out and were being heard. There were many feel good moments, but it was exhausting. To exacerbate the stress, I realized that I was using up all my personal days in my teaching job, which would have an adverse effect on my pension.

EIGHTEEN
Contact Visits (early 1980s)

Gene stayed at Sing Sing for a short time and then was moved to Green Haven.

The transfer from Sing Sing to Green Haven was daunting. In miles, Green Haven was not too much farther than Sing Sing. Although there were only twelve prisons in New York State at that time, most of the existing facilities were way up north. Auburn, Attica, and Clinton were names that chilled my bones. Green Haven had such a soothing sound to it, and it was not an eight-hour drive.

The tattoo on Gene's arm read "Lucky." Luck is a relative term.

Gene tried to send me directions. He intently watched the road, turns, and landmarks as he was transported from one place to the other. Really, it never entered his mind that I had the capability to figure it out on my own. Children were permitted at Green Haven; I chose not to bring my girls. The visiting conditions were certainly not geared for family bonding.

On my first visit, I had decided to check it out by myself. I was astounded. After experiencing contact visits in Sing Sing, I was back to restricted visitation. I walked into a room with a long table down the middle and a screen from the ceiling to the table top. Upon entering, I found an opening with just enough room to allow me to kiss my husband. Then we proceeded to opposite sides of the table to take our chairs. We could reach in and touch fingertips. Again, there were people right next to us, on either side. My whole body was shaking with anger. I decided right then that my children would not be allowed to visit. It would be like taking them to a zoo where they could see their daddy in a cage.

Since visiting Gene in Sing Sing, the girls looked forward to seeing him. Again, I had to explain to them that Daddy loved and missed them, but they were not going to be able to see him for a while. Of course, the children did not understand. Why should they be expected to? As an adult I could not wrap my head around this kind of reasoning.

Why should my children suffer for the wrongs of their father? I am not saying that children should be compelled to endure prison visits. It should remain a decision made by a parent for all the right reasons. Is it in the best interest of the child? Is the incarcerated person fulfilling the role of a caring parent, to the degree he or she is able? Is the experience positive for the child? All this must be taken into consideration. But for the state to ensure that these visits are demeaning for all is deplorable. If it is safe for my child to have a contact visit in one facility, why is it prohibited in all the others?

The easy answer is: Why not?

Sing Sing was the only prison in New York State to have contact visits. Where was the logic? Every person arrested and sentenced to a year or longer was sent to the Sing Sing reception center. The people in that visiting room ran the gamut from white-collar criminals to serial killers. If it was safe for us to have contact with our prisoner here, what changed when they were sent elsewhere?

The key word here is *logic*.

Once more, I was faced with an injustice. Where was the humanity? A question I asked myself again and again during my journey as a prison wife.

By now, I was a reluctant regular on the Fortune Society speaking circuit, talking about the effects of incarceration on those doing their time on the outside. My mentor and guru, David Rothenberg, encouraged me to use my grown-up voice and confront the system.

And so, with my newly borrowed confidence and power, and with David and Kenny supporting me, I put my anger to good use. I was now about to go on a crusade to bring contact visits to all jails and prisons in New York State.

With trembling knees and aware that I had a slight speech impediment, a hatred for public speaking, and feeling of intimidation in the presence of authority figures, I spoke before the New York State Assembly and Senate, the Commissioner of Corrections, wardens as they were then known, sheriffs, and anyone else who had ears and might be able to sway the system. I wrote an article about contact visits for the *Fortune News*, the newsletter of the Fortune Society. It was reprinted in the *Congressional Record* and, believe it or not, in the *Weekly Reader*, a newspaper that was widely distributed to schools.

My daughters received this edition in their classrooms and came home quite excited that my article was there for all their classmates to see. It was an impersonal piece; nothing was said that might embarrass my children, but I realized that I was exposing my whole family in ways that always gave me a twinge of discomfort.

A warden, whose name I do not remember, informed me that, although only a very small percentage of people needed this kind of security, I would not see contact visits expanded in my lifetime.

This man passed away many years ago. I am alive, and there are for now contact visits in every prison in New York State. When the Nassau County Jail did away with their phone systems, I was invited to the celebration of the opening of the new contact visiting room. Finally, the Plexiglas was taken down, the phones removed, and the people who came to visit could touch their loved ones. They sat across from each other and could have private conversations without the fear that each word was being monitored. Children were finally allowed the "privilege" of visiting.

The big fear was that families would bring in contraband. No doubt some misguided people are guilty of this crime (and they do usually get caught and arrested); few grandmas, mothers, fathers, or wives even consider this. We are just so happy that our loved ones are in a situation where, we hope, they are not exposed to drugs and alcohol. It is unthinkable to most of us to do anything that might jeopardize their sobriety or safety. I maintain that the staff tends to be more responsible for the contraband than the visitors.

Many jurisdictions have implemented video visitation.

New York State is exploring this idea. The premise is that since it is difficult for many families to travel to those far-away prisons, it would enable loved ones to see each other, via technology. Or, if someone is physically incapacitated, it could be an option. It would also be a cost-saver for corrections, eliminating the need for visiting room staff and security checkpoints. And of course, this will avoid having "outsiders" invade their domains.

Did I mention that the reason those high walls surround the prison is as much to keep *us* out as to keep the inmates in?

Many of the jurisdictions that have already implemented video visiting are charging families exorbitant fees to access the technology, while still requiring them to travel to distant sites. What the facility saves on staffing, the family spends on the privilege of being allowed to see their loved one's faces on a TV monitor. I have been told that in some places the camera angles only show the top of the head.

Although some of the reasons for the implementation of video visitation seem valid enough, it is a slippery slope. It is likely that once this becomes policy for all the right reasons, we will see the "privilege" of person-to-person visitation chipped away. Even the brief embrace at the beginning and end of each visit will be eliminated. The fight will have to be won all over again.

With the available technology, visits with psychologists, parole boards, and attorneys are being "Skyped."

There are other more humane solutions to the contact problem. Moving people in prison to facilities closer to home would help—as would greater use of work-release and community-based treatment programs.

During the hearings we attended in the 1980s regarding visitation, some discussion centered on conjugal visits. As Kenny put it so succinctly, these visits should not be just to "conjugate." We stressed the importance of furloughs that would allow people, separated from society for years, to gradually readjust to the real world.

Most people will be coming home after living in an alternate universe of violence, dehumanization, and isolation. We open the prison doors, give them a few bucks and a bus ticket, and say, "Welcome home. Now you are on your own." The practice does not acknowledge that the spouse and children have also been living in an alternate universe. How can they live happily ever after?

New York State did introduce the Family Reunion Program (FRP), used mostly in maximum security prisons. Trailers are set up inside the prison walls, where family—wives, parents, children, or siblings—can spend a few days, in *near* normal conditions. Families can bring food, videos, and a bit of the outside world with, them, and—sorry Kenny—husbands and wives can conjugate.

Our men and the growing number of women who are in prison will one day be coming out to their neighborhoods but first, if they are lucky, to their families. Allowing them to gradually reenter this real world might help everyone learn to adjust more effectively than confining them in conditions intended to replicate real life. It is not real when your movement and choices are still controlled.

In my informed opinion, the primary purpose of the trailer visits is to encourage long-termers to behave, because an infraction will deprive them of this perk. Meanwhile, it is better than nothing.

Recently a bill has been introduced in New York State to do away with the Family Reunion Program. As of September 2017, Shirley was still allowed the dubious honor of shopping for three days' worth of approved food items, lugging the heavy packages up to the prison, and going through a rigorous screening process. Then she and her son could spend a few days together in a trailer where they could cook together, watch TV, and perhaps play with puzzles. At the end of the visit the premises had to be spotless and every utensil accounted for.

If you would like to know more about the Family Reunion Program in New York, the website of the Department of Corrections and Community Supervision will tell you all you need to know. All, that is, except the way it feels to know that when these visits end, your loved one is going back to the reality of a prison cell.

NINETEEN
Green Haven (circa 1967)

Gene and I were settled into our routine. He was doing his time: reading, playing cards and chess, exercising, and trying to stay healthy with the food I sent in his thirty-five-pound monthly packages. I also kept him supplied with vitamins I ordered from a mail order company. Gene would tell me in his letters what he required for his next package and I, the dutiful wife, wasted not a moment but ran out to the neighborhood supermarket, with shopping list in hand, to comply with his every culinary wish. There was not much I could do to comfort Gene, so these packages were a declaration of love.

I kept a box by the kitchen cabinet, filling it with sardines, peanut butter, crackers, and other favorites so that on the day of the visit, I would have everything ready to put into shopping bags for my trip upstate.

Traveling to Green Haven became an every-weekend ritual.

Carpooling with families I met along the way made the drive bearable. Long Islanders Cathy Gibalaro, "Wipsy," and I were regulars on the Taconic Parkway, driving to Stormville, New York, to visit our respective husbands. Edna and a few others often joined us, but we were the core. We were labeled the "three moms from L.I." Amongst us there were eight children with a daddy in prison.

We would chatter all the way up to the prison, laughing, sharing stories of our children, and the difficulty of raising them with their father in prison. About halfway to the prison, we would make a pit stop. We would find a diner where we could freshen up and have a cup of coffee to go with the rolls or pastry we usually brought with us.

We disguised our angst by laughing, wondering out loud what our fellow patrons would think if they knew that one of us was married to a murderer, another married to a rapist, and the third married to a lowly thief.

The packages in the car always came with a homemade red sauce made by our in-car chef, Cathy. She would make the yummy, authentic Italian sauce, pour it into brand name jars, and, with the help of an accomplice, reseal them. We never got caught bringing it in, and I never figured out how she did it. I suppose the statute of limitations has expired, and dear Cathy has long since passed away. We were quite innocent. The strongest thing in that sauce was the red pepper. We would have died before we introduced any illegal substance. We went to bed each night grateful with the thought that our husbands were not using drugs or alcohol. If they were, it was not supplied by us.

Our husbands, who were allowed to cook in their common areas, were on the same tier, so they could and did share the goodies we schlepped. At least Green Haven did not have Sing Sing's hill.

After these visits, we got back into the car and barely uttered a word on the trip back home. Each of us was dealing with our pain silently. The sadness and sense of separation were too much to put into words.

The parole board hearing was creeping up on us. With his good time intact, Gene was eligible for parole after serving only two years of his minimum two-and-a-half year sentence. As much as I wanted him to come home to us, I felt much trepidation. I did not want to return to the insanity, the walking on eggs, the not knowing whether Dr. Jekyll or Mr. Hyde would be sleeping in my bed.

To be honest, I was not ready to relinquish my role as head of my household. But I did want my gentle lover back. I had stacks of letters assuring me that he was going to devote his life to loving and caring for me and the girls. He would live the rest of his life trying to make up for the pain he caused us.

I had no reason to believe that we would not have a happy ending. The letters and visits reassured me and Gene had been, to the best of my knowledge, clean and sober for his two years of incarceration.

TWENTY
Reasonable Assurance (1969)

The Fortune Society had been invited to speak at a public event in Smithtown, New York, a location forty minutes away from Hempstead. I gave my usual speech, stressing how the impact of incarceration affects a family. This time, there was a caveat. I mentioned that Gene was going to appear before the Board of Parole Commissioners, who had the power to hold him in prison until he completed his maximum sentence of seven years. He needed to meet certain requirements before they would even consider releasing him. A suitable residence and reasonable assurance of a job were basic necessities before they would even consider anyone for release.

Lo and behold, in the audience was the owner of a computer school located right in Smithtown. She was looking for a teacher for her school and was moved by my words—enough to go to Green Haven and interview Gene. She was so impressed with him that she offered him the job on the spot.

He not only had reasonable assurance of a job, but the offer of a job that had substance.

In New York, the prisoner usually appeared before three parole commissioners. He or she was given a few minutes to answer some questions and plead his or her case. Supposedly these commissioners had read the inmate's file before arriving at the prison. The file would consist of disciplinary infractions, psych reports, the presentencing report compiled by probation, letters of support from supporters—and letters from victims and perhaps law enforcement opposing the inmate's release. All things pertinent to his or her past and present were supposed to be in that file. How closely this file is scrutinized is a matter of opinion.

In New York, all that information currently is window dressing. In 2017 the only thing parole commissioners base their decisions on is the nature of the crime, something that will never change.

For more about parole, I suggest you read *Geranium Justice: The Other Side of the Table* by Barbara Hansen Treen.

But this is now. That was then. In 1969, Gene was eligible for a parole hearing. He was seen by the board on a Tuesday, but we did not get the results until Friday. They were a grueling three days. He and Bill, Edna's husband, appeared before the same parole board. Edna heard before I did that Bill was given a go-home date. Although I was happy for Edna, I was feeling a little envious. I didn't expect that they would release Gene—yet.

My Fortune family warned me that Gene had gotten his break in court; I should be grateful for that but not expect another miracle. I was resigned that he might be held another year or even two. Hope, but don't expect!

By now I had become a very verbal critic of the system. I had taken advantage of every opportunity to expose, complain about, and advocate against each and every wrong I witnessed.

Because we were always concerned about retaliation, I did nothing without Gene's knowledge. He encouraged me to speak out, so I did. There were consequences for my big mouth. It went from the absurd to the ridiculous. Some of the affronts were minor, like the time I went on a visit and they could not find him. Excuse me. I know that he disappeared on the street, but how could you lose him in a maximum security prison?

Or the count might be wrong. We would wait as long as it took and lose hours of our precious visiting time. Then there was the inconsistency in what was acceptable to bring in a package. One month something would be perfectly appropriate, and the next month it would be disallowed, a waste of our precious dollars. Or a visit might be cut short, for no apparent reason; of course, there was no recourse. I never let a slight go by without asking to see the warden, threatening to go to the press, or just issuing a complaint. And that was for the minor nuisances. For the really important issues, I was going public.

But the miracle happened. Gene made his first board. Kenny had no doubt that they got rid of Gene to "shut Barbara up."

They still have not been able to do that.

TWENTY-ONE
On Parole (1969)

With no preparation or psychiatric help, homecoming promised to be horrific. There is always a list of dos and don'ts for parolees. Gene had a 7:00 P.M. curfew, with an exception for work and AA meetings. He was not allowed to drive; of course, alcohol was not permitted. He couldn't change his residence or leave the area without written permission. He could not consort with anyone who had a criminal record.

The first few months were the honeymoon phase. Gene started his job at the computer school and, as always, he impressed his employers with his skills and work ethic. Because he was on parole, the driving restriction was a nightmare. In our suburban area, public transportation was almost nonexistent, particularly inter-county. We lived in Nassau County, and Gene's job was in Suffolk County. I drove him to work before my teaching day started, then backtracked to my school where I spent the day teaching seven-year-old children, preparing lessons, correcting papers, attending faculty meetings, meeting with parents, and so on. Then, depending on Gene's schedule, I went out east again, often during rush hour, and we would drive home. Sometimes, particularly when Gene worked evening shifts, my father would take over the chauffeuring duty.

Here I was, still doing time with him. Now it was parole time. Mr. Levine, our parole officer, was extremely fond of Gene. Not so much me.

Life was getting stressful. Commuting was wearing me down. Although my mother and father provided child care, my girls and I needed bonding time. The children were always a high priority for me, and the commuting time was interfering with parenting time. It seemed as though all my nonworking hours were spent driving Gene. On the Saturdays that Gene worked, the girls and I made an adventure out of picking Daddy up. We would go to his school, play with the computers, and then go across the street to Friendly's for an ice-cream specialty.

Within a few months of his being home, Gene's employers set about opening another school. This would be much closer to home and accessible by bus. They offered Gene the position of director of their Mineola school. He agreed to it but, as was his pattern, he retreated into his paranoia just when things were looking up.

I could tell that he was relapsing, although his job performance was not affected. He told me that his bosses were taking advantage of him, that he was not appreciated. He began to repeat his old mantra—he was not going to be somebody's flunky. Anytime something good was on the horizon, Gene found a way to sabotage it.

It started subtly but progressed rapidly. One day, he told me that he would be staying late at work and that he planned to pick up the keys for a second car. "Why should you have to go out at night to pick me up? Fuck parole. The parole officer isn't the one who has to ride the buses." He had convinced himself that he was perfectly able to drive and that no one had the right to tell him otherwise.

As much as I disapproved, I could not physically stop him. I was not about to snitch to parole. Let the chips fall where they may. It was his decision, and the consequences would fall on him.

In all honesty, I was relieved to relinquish the role of chauffeur.

So he started violating parole by driving. Then, he did not come right home from work, breaking curfew. He started drinking, although at first he tried hard to conceal it from me. I could see the old pattern emerging. He was hiding the bottles, looking for an excuse to start an argument so that he could justify walking out. I realized that if I let myself, I would relapse into the cycle of violence.

Brenda and Tina were seeing a counselor who specialized in treating families of alcoholics. They were also attending an Alatot meeting. I was in therapy and attending Al-Anon meetings. We were working hard at healing. Gene was attending AA meetings, in retrospect more to satisfy me and parole than to truly seek sobriety. Still, he was going regularly. He was reading the Big Book and was working the steps. I was on a pink cloud.

We had a six-month clean and sober party, with cake and high hopes.

It didn't last. Once the drinking started again, it couldn't have. All bets were off. I was fearful of directly stirring the beast, so I went to the people with the power.

I contacted Mr. Levine, which was tricky. There was so much at stake for me. Drinking brought out the violent side of Gene, and I wanted parole to intervene. They had the authority and, I thought, the mandate to condemn this behavior.

It didn't happen. Mr. Levine continued visiting Gene at home and enjoyed playing pool in our basement—on the pool table I bought so that Gene did not have to go out to bars to play pool. He invited neighbors and colleagues to play with him. The girls quickly learned the game. These were friendly, social gatherings. That worked for about a week-and-a-half.

Gene missed the ambiance of the smoke-filled, loud, neon lit, sawdust-on-the-floors camaraderie he found in gin mills. Clever Gene found a way to get the best of both of his worlds. He practiced the art of compromise.

He would continue shooting pool with his drinking buddies, and, at closing time, he brought his pool-playing drunks to our house to finish the game. This, mind you, was the house where his wife and children were sleeping.

Our parole officer kept enjoying a relaxing game of pool during his home visits. Gene knew how to be a perfect host. I almost expected them to whip out a six pack. When Gene turned on the charm, he could make you think that orange was purple and that there was no such thing as climate change.

I began to lose trust in my own judgment. Most everyone around him thought that Gene was doing well. He was still flourishing at work. My attempt to alert Mr. Levine didn't work; he accused me of exaggerating.

Was I imagining things? Hell no! A few years back, Gene's psychiatrist had the same response to my warnings. That was only weeks before the murder.

Gene was drinking and doing a good job of hiding it. But I knew what I knew.

Kenny Jackson knew that I was not delusional. He went with me to speak with a parole supervisor who was not quite as bewitched by Gene.

The parole board finally decided he was in violation. The honeymoon was officially over. I lost count of how many rearrests there were. Gene became known as a frequent flier. Our life was now a series of parole violations, police contacts, automobile accidents, and domestic violence complaints from me.

The staff at the Nassau County Jail told me that they had a cell there with his name on it. Some of these arrests led to more state time. Some led to mandatory rehab. We all knew that jail was not the answer. It only exacerbated his problems. But when he was allowed rehab, he was just biding his time before he went back behind bars.

Of course, I was disappointed and hurt that the drinking continued. My head told me, "Stop it, go, run, run as far as you can." But here I was again performing like a robot, almost as though I was programmed, still following the old patterns. Each time I saw him in his orange jumpsuit, or his prison greens, all reason disappeared and I was back on that merry-go-round of denial. When he was in jail and sober, he appeared vulnerable and needy, which gave me permission to rationalize that this was going to be the last time. Over and over, he conned me into believing that he had hit his bottom and that he was going to return to AA and really work the program. I'll give him this. He never once blamed me for calling the cops on him. He recognized that when he was out of control, I needed to protect myself from him.

So out of misguided love, hope, and/or overwhelming fear, I continued to do my time with him.

TWENTY-TWO
Friends of Fortune (1972)

Most of Gene's violent episodes were predictable. They came when he was drinking. Still, as is the case with many alcoholics, the only thing that was predictable was the unpredictability.

Gene continued attending AA meetings. He put himself on Antabuse, a drug that makes you severely ill if you consume any alcohol. Each morning Gene would come to the kitchen table with his cup of coffee and swallow his magic pill. I would smile and feel safe, kiss him goodbye, and leave for work, content in the knowledge that I would have a sober husband when I came home—until the day he wasn't.

The Fortune Society was spreading out to Long Island and to New Jersey. Here on LI we had an active group of formerly incarcerated men who were willing to take the reins and grow Fortune into the suburbs. We had an office, a staff, and lots of enthusiasm. We even had a van to drive families to upstate prisons. Ronnie Daigneault was leader of the pack, with Warren, Mike, or Tyrone riding shotgun.

They were an interesting group, with many years of prison time among them. Mixed in with our former con men and crooks were some of the pillars of society. In order to fulfill their pledge to become involved in social causes, IBM helped with technology. They "loaned" us Bob Goggins, who was part of Friends of Fortune. Bob's wife, Kathy, also volunteered with us. We had Vista volunteers, young people who chose to give some years of their lives to better conditions for others.

One of our dearest supporters was Dorothy Fisher, a member of the Garden City Community Church. She and the members of her church were the backbone of our toy drives for many years. We were always able to count on our many community partners to fill in wherever they were needed, be it driving a van to a prison or helping in the office.

Although I was the liaison between Fortune in New York City and the group on Long Island, I found it difficult to slow Ronnie down. His wants did not always jibe with the wishes of our group.

The day Gene's Antabuse caper collapsed was the day the warriors of Friends of Fortune were going to use that van to travel upstate to share their successes with a group of still-incarcerated men. Gene was going to accompany them. I was so proud. I didn't expect to come home to a falling-down drunk. Oops! The pill he had been taking the few previous days was a plain old aspirin. With no Antabuse in his system, Gene decided he would rather sit in a bar than go on that rickety old van with people who were trying to put their lives together. When he got home, I was so disgusted that I told him he needed to leave. Again.

He did not lash out at me or beg me to forgive me. Instead, he had a new ploy. He had gotten his hands on a gun. He lay down on the carpet by my feet, with the gun propped by his head, and threatened to kill himself. Instead of kicking his hand so that the gun would go off, I begged, "Please, Gene, don't. Don't kill yourself." He didn't. He willingly gave me the gun.

My father turned it in, and Gene checked into another rehab.

This began another series of rehabs and re-incarcerations. I knew that I had to make a decision, as scared and confused as I was. There was no way that I could continue on this roller coaster. If he was going to kill me, so be it. I was tired and defeated. The words of my current therapist rang in my head. "If you knew there was a live stick of dynamite in your living room, would you stay there with it and watch it get ready to explode, or would you run as far from it as possible?"

Put that way, it made simple sense. Get the hell as far away from the blast as quickly as you can.

TWENTY-THREE
Fire (1974)

Leaving was scary on so many levels. I was totally sick and tired of being sick and tired. I wanted out of this non-marriage. I wanted away from this insanity. I could not get rid of the beast and hold onto the man. It was suggested by many, including my therapist, that I change my Social Security number and just run, just leave.

I couldn't. I was not going to leave my parents, my home, my friends, and look for work under a new identity. My daughters were not going to have to live in shadows. If someone needed to go, it would have to be him.

The push-pull was complicated, but at the heart of it was fear. Each time I tried to leave, it led to a catastrophe. In my heart I did not think he would kill me, but my head knew better than to trust my heart. He was not going to let me go easily. What I saw as love was really power and control!

After all, I had left him once. Then he killed his father. And then there was this. How many times had he told me that if I left him, he would kill me or burn our house down?

Then there was that part of me that remembered the poetry and roses in our courtship and marriage. But, I could no longer allow myself the luxury of thinking that he would stop drinking because he loved me.

Push! Pull!

Despite all of that, I went ahead and got another order of protection, knowing that it might not be worth much. Still, he was again ordered to stay away from me.

Then came the night of the fire.

It was late summer. The girls and I were still on our summer break. It had been a stress-filled two months. Our daughters were entitled to a normal summer—going to the beach, to the town pool, on day trips and picnics. We managed to do all this while dodging Gene. I knew he was out there. I saw him in my rearview mirror. He would always be lurking.

One day, when my car wouldn't start in my school parking lot, the custodian opened the hood to jump the battery. The battery had been removed.

Even though I had changed the locks on all my doors, I knew that he had gotten into the house. Things were moved around. Small items were missing.

He threw pebbles at Brenda's window. When she opened it, he begged her to ask Mommy to give him a cup of tea or at least a teabag. Do you know how hard it was to say "No" and to explain to Brenda why I couldn't give it to him?

Again, the drinking had escalated, and I had no doubt that despite a stay-away order, he would continue returning to our house. I could sense a heightening of despair in him. The more I avoided him, the more determined he became.

He stalked me, followed me, and harassed me. He begged and threatened me. I called the cops, and then he would behave—for a while.

I had my father install an alarm system throughout my house so that at the push of a button the police and my father would be notified. I had to use it on occasion. Gene would go to jail for a few months, then write to tell me how sorry he was and that he would never do it again.

He would be released from jail and really try sobriety for a while. Back to AA. It was a recurring cycle, but I never let my guard down.

Hope, but don't expect.

The drinking always started again,

Alcoholism is an insidious disease, which keeps right on progressing, even if the drinking stops. You can remain dry for ten years, but when you pick up the next drink your body reacts as though you never stopped.

Once I realized that he was drinking again, I refused to allow him near me or the girls. With every sip of booze he took, his resentment built.

At a certain point, I could tell that the cauldron was about to boil over. He called me and I heard the slur in his voice. Once more, I knew it was time to run.

I brought the girls to have a sleep over with their grandparents, and I went to find sanctuary with Dee. As expected, through the process of elimination, he found me. There were only so many places I could hide. Damn! I was so tired of running.

He was beside himself with frustration. How dare I? He knew Dee's phone number and called incessantly. "Come home, Barbara. I love you. We can work things out. I can't live without you."

Sometimes we let the phone ring without answering it, but more often than not, I would speak to him because we knew that while he was on the phone, he could not be right outside. That was way before the advent of cell phones.

When we picked up the phone that last time, he said, "Barbara, you have to come home. The house is on fire."

"I don't care," I said. "Let it burn."

And so it did.

But we did call the police. David Chaisson (Davy) bicycled over and was hanging onto a baseball bat, just in case.

Davy became part of our family when he was released from Green Haven. He was a lost soul, lacking in education and social graces but trying hard to give up the life of petty crimes that caused his frequent interaction with the police. Gene had mentored him when they met at Green Haven.

When Davy was released from prison, he chose to come to Long Island to be with "the winners" at Friends of Fortune. He really was tired of his lifestyle. He hoped that he could find something different. Gene and I discussed his coming to live with our family until he got established. Parole approved his residence with us, despite both their rap sheets. Chalk one up for parole.

Davy quickly became part of our extended family of repenting thieves and misfits. He perceived himself as the protector of the Allan family, and his loyalty to me was unflinching. He never hesitated to use his scrawny body as a shield if he thought that Gene was going to be a threat to me. So he brought his only weapon, a baseball bat, and risked going back to jail.

It wasn't long before Gene showed up. Shouting at the locked door, "Barbara, I know you're in there. Get your ass out here. I need to talk to you. Dee, tell her to get the fuck out here. I love you, Barb. You have to go home. The house is burning." The begging and cursing was interspersed with sobs.

Meanwhile, Dee was trying to hide me, telling me to get down on the floor. "Don't let him see you." She was concerned for me and for her own children, who were upstairs in their bedroom. Davy was pacing and mumbling, "Just let me get my hands on him."

I was trying to hold him back while staying away from the windows, terrified that he would see me. We didn't know if he had a weapon. Finally, Gene kicked in the door and attempted to enter Dee's house. By then we could hear the sirens of the approaching police cars.

Dee was able to have Gene arrested for breaking and entering.

I walked through that burned out house, holding onto my sanity by repeating the Serenity Prayer:

God, grant me the serenity to accept the things I cannot change.

The courage to change those things I can,

And the wisdom to know the difference.

The odor of smoke was overwhelming. What was not burned was saturated with water and smoke. I was in a state of shock. So many of my life's milestones were destroyed. The poems and stories I wrote as a girl and young woman had been stored in the basement. My high school and college yearbooks, my daughters' baby books, my pictures and letters—all were lost to me. These were things that could never be replaced.

Accept the things I cannot change!

My neighbor had seen Gene breaking into the house, carrying a gas can. The fire originated in the dining room. Our dog, Rex, was in the house. When the firefighters broke down the front door, Rex was able to find his way to the sanctuary of my parents' home. Our gerbils died.

My insurance company arranged for us to stay in a motel and promised that they would have a trailer placed on our property to house us until I could rebuild.

Within a few days it was determined that I was not entitled to collect on my fully paid insurance policy. Gene was the co-owner of the house, and he deliberately set the fire so they did not have to honor the terms. If I hoped to appeal this decision, it was in my best interest if Gene was not charged with arson.

I called Kenny Jackson. He came immediately, as he always did when my world was in a tailspin. We met with the fire marshal. My neighbor did not verify what he had seen, so although Gene went back to prison on the breaking and entering charge and a parole violation, he was not charged with arson.

Even without the eyewitness testimony, it was apparent that the fire was arson. The insurance company was going to do their own investigation. They stopped paying our living expenses, and I could not afford to stay in a motel any longer.

We all moved in with my mother and father. I needed to get back to work as soon as possible. Tina and Brenda needed some stability. This was not to happen just yet.

A few weeks later I was admitted to the hospital. I had been bleeding internally and needed surgery to remove a tumor. To add to my stress, I discovered that I was almost three months pregnant. Pregnant, homeless, and emotionally bankrupt, I needed to make a hard decision.

The surgery terminated my pregnancy. Gene never knew that I had been pregnant. There was no reason to tell him.

I remained in the hospital for over a week. Hempstead General Hospital was so overcrowded that for a time I was not assigned a room and had to convalesce in the hall. I didn't know how much lower I could sink, emotionally or physically, but I fought to hold onto my sanity because of Tina and Brenda. They needed their mother now more than ever. Gene could take everything else, but he was not going to take me away from my children.

When I was released from the hospital, I joined the girls, hoping these living arrangements would be for a short time. It was close quarters. There were two bedrooms and one bath, but we tried to manage. I slept in the basement and the girls shared a room. We did not know how long it would take me to get the finances to allow me to rebuild.

Because of the surgery, I was on a six-week sick leave from work. As soon as I was physically able, Marjorie picked us up, and we went on a road trip to her part-time residence in Florida. Marge had to leave teaching for medical reasons, but she was always there for me. Had canes, did travel.

The trip was a much-needed tonic. We stopped at Disney World, and we went to St. Augustine to drink from the Fountain of Youth. Marjorie was very generous. Always my angel.

When I returned home it was obvious to me that there would not be an insurance settlement in the foreseeable future. We again moved into my childhood home. It was crowded.

My colleague and friend, Allyn Eckstein, offered to rent us space in her larger home. She was recently divorced, and she said that she would like the company. This brought us to a living space far from the girls' school district but close to where I worked. My principal, Charlie Triolo, arranged it so that Tina and Brenda could attend our school. Tina was in fourth grade and Brenda in third. For a few months we lived with Allyn and her two sons. Everyone got along well and the girls had an easy transition to their new school, thanks to the sensitivity of my colleagues at George Washington Elementary School.

But it had to be temporary. At the end of the school year we moved back to my parents' home and the children to their home school.

I was struggling financially. On top of our living expenses, I still was expected to pay the mortgage and taxes on my uninhabitable shell of a house. But I persisted. Finally, nearly five years later, I was awarded a fraction of what the insurance policy should have paid, and a third of that went to my attorney.

We did a quick deed and Gene signed what was left of the house over to me. I now had the incentive to rebuild. With a loan from my Aunt Francis, and taking the maximum allowable from my retirement fund, I was able to rebuild. The girls and I moved back to 10 Foster Place.

TWENTY-FOUR
Divorce (1975)

I called George Schatz, Gene's murder trial attorney, to plan my divorce. I had no intention of alerting Gene.

Our opportunity came. After going on a binge, Gene decided he needed a vacation, ostensibly to visit his brother. I gladly drove him to the bus station and hummed a few bars of "Thank God and Greyhound You're Gone."

We had already placed an ad in an east-end paper saying that I would no longer be responsible for the debts of Herman Gene Allan and expressed my intent to divorce him.

And I did.

He left without dreaming that I would go to court. I asked nothing from him, and I was able to honestly tell the judge that I had no idea where he was. After almost eleven years of hell, I was granted an uncontested divorce. I even had a party to celebrate. All my Al-Anon friends were there.

The marriage was over. At least for me.

Gene, of course, returned from his wanderings. He had made his way down south, hitch hiking, riding boxcars, and doing whatever he needed to maintain his lifestyle as a drunk. He was arrested in Arkansas and was forced to detox in a jail cell, where he suffered from hallucinations and severe pain. Again, he made the decision to return home, go to AA, and try his best to stay sober.

During one of those dry spells, he came over for a cup of coffee and a dose of honesty. We sat at the kitchen table. He had a cup of very sweet coffee in his steady hand. I had a cup of black, strong coffee in my shaking hand. I closed my eyes and in one breath said, "Gene, I need to tell you that we are divorced." We did not make eye contact.

It took no time for him to say, rather casually, "No, we are not. Impossible! We are not divorced. You are my wife 'til death do us part."

I explained to him how it came to be. He in turn explained to me, as though speaking to a child, that it was only a piece of paper and we were not divorced. So there!

Well, it did go better than expected. There were no histrionics, no drama, no threats, no fist banging. Just quiet denial.

We finished our coffee like two civilized people. He walked out the door, turned, walked back to me, kissed me on the forehead, and said, "You are now and always will be my wife."

I sat there for a moment stunned, though I do not know why I was surprised.

We might have had a lousy marriage, but we had a pretty interesting divorce. I was legally no longer anyone's wife, and I decided to live the part. I got a bumper sticker proclaiming that happiness is being divorced. I dated, even had a marriage proposal.

Gene phoned me every evening. He tore the bumper sticker off my car. He begged, and he cried that he loved me and would never hurt me, that I was all that mattered, blah, blah, blah.

I admit that there were times when he wore me down.

He moved into a rooming house in Garden City. I allowed him to sneak me in there now and again. I still remembered the good times. But I would not let him near my house.

TWENTY-FIVE
Sober at Last (1978)

It was Friday, January 13, 1978, during an ice storm, at about 10:00 P.M. when my phone rang. It was a very drunk, very sick Gene. He was living in a boarding house about five miles from us. He was crying and moaning that he had to go to detox. Would I come and get him?

"No," I said. Every part of me was shaking right along with him. I believed that I was feeling the same pain he was feeling. "If you wanted to go out for a drink, you would find a way. I suggest you use those skills to get you wherever you need to go."

I *was* conflicted. My mind turned back to that night a few years earlier, when a hungover Gene threw pebbles at Brenda's window to get our attention, looking for tea and sympathy.

"Please give me a tea bag," he begged.

"No." Once again I had to close my heart to him.

I knew that the definition of insanity is doing the same thing over and over and expecting different results. I was taught in Al-Anon to mind my own business and not to accept the unacceptable. I read and reread in my *One Day at a Time.* I found the page that said, "You have the right to a decent life, and no one has a right to take that away from you." And I became a believer. When I hung up the phone,

I repeated the serenity prayer and went to sleep.

Gene found his way to Freeport Hospital that night. He convinced one of his housemates to drive him. After a few days of detox, he signed himself into South Oaks Hospital for rehab. There he said that he had a "spiritual awakening," that led him back to the rooms of AA, for the first time without being mandated or manipulative. Now he went because he was sick and tired of being sick and tired.

I minded my own business and went about my life. I did not visit him. However, once he was allowed phone calls, he called me. The girls and I continued with our therapy and Al-Anon. I was invited to speak at Al-Anon meetings and group anniversaries. I was honored to be asked to be the speaker at the South Oaks Al-Anon group anniversary. I facilitated a twelve-step group in Westbury.

After leaving rehab, Gene made his ninety meetings in ninety days. He found a home group, asked someone to sponsor him, and actually tried working the program.

Gene stopped using alcohol at the age of forty-one.

He went to closed meetings, open meetings, Big Book meetings, and twelve-step meetings. Because this is a disease of the attitude, it took Gene many more years to achieve true sobriety. Dealing with a dry Gene was no nirvana. The underlying psychosis was not eradicated. Gene's moods were still erratic, and his behavior unpredictable. But there was no overt violence.

TWENTY-SIX
California, Here We Come (1977)

During all of this, we did not live in a vacuum, and life was still happening to us. Some of it was interesting and fun. Some of it was bizarre. I was in survival mode when we took our cross-country bus trip. The idea came to me when a teacher at the girls' school suggested that we drive to California with him and his daughter. They had a trailer and were heading west for summer vacation. Although Ed and I had dated a few times, I did not think I was ready for that much togetherness, but the idea stuck with me.

Greyhound was advertising a "get off, get back on" bus trip at an affordable price. In the summer of 1977 I took off with my twelve- and thirteen-year- old princesses, and we boarded a bus at the Greyhound terminal in New York. Our final destination was Los Angeles.

We had amazing adventures. There was no dark shadow hanging over our heads and we took advantage of the great things our country had to offer. We stopped in Chicago to visit Lori, their friend and our neighbor who was visiting her brother in the windy city. We spent a few days exploring the city. I had lived in Chicago for about a year, when my father was stationed there during the war. It was interesting to revisit the school I attended and to see the nearby stockyards, a Chicago landmark, which gave the city the distinction of being known as "hog butcher for the world."

After a few days we got back on a bus. Our next scheduled stop was Tempe, Arizona. We chose that as a destination because one of our fellow travelers told us that they had opened a water park in the desert. Our visit there also lasted a few days. We visited the Big Surf Water Park, which had opened in 1969, an oasis in the desert.

The summer heat was extremely intense during our visit. We decided to go for an early morning horseback ride, before the sun had a chance to cause too much discomfort. We had checked into this particular hotel because it was within walking distance to a stable, and we all loved to ride. By the time we walked to the stable, the heat had intensified and we decided to take pity on the horses. As disappointed as the girls were, compassion won and we fed the horses a carrot and started the walk back to the motel. Though the walk was less than a mile, I was worried that we would suffer heat exhaustion; when a kind-hearted gentleman stopped and offered us a ride, we gratefully hopped into his air conditioned car, totally negating the message that I had drilled into my girls. "Never, ever take a ride from a stranger" — except when it was the lesser of two evils, one of which was dying from heat stroke.

We went to The Grand Canyon to see one of the wonders of the world. We stayed overnight at a cabin on the canyon grounds, where we explored at leisure and soaked in the beauty.

Our next stop was Wyoming, where we went to see a rodeo. We stayed at a ranch where the girls met some boys their ages, which was a highlight for them. Meeting and getting to know people of different backgrounds and from different parts of the country was the icing on the cake.

We finally reached our destination in California. Terry, a Prison Families Anonymous member who had relocated to San Fernando Valley, welcomed us with a generous heart. Her house had plenty of room for us. It was home base while we ventured out to see southern California. We stayed a few days in Santa Monica, where my cousin Neil lived at the time. We went to Knott's Berry Farm, where we went on all the rides and stocked up on boysenberry jam.

We almost lost Brenda crossing the border from Mexico. We had wandered down to Tijuana for an afternoon visit. It was an exciting place, a typical border town, and so close to San Diego that I could not resist. It was definitely a city sustained by tourists, but I wanted the girls to get a little flavor of being in a different country. At the border crossing on the way back, an agent singled Brenda out and pulled her away from us. My heart stopped, and I think Tina is still traumatized. Because Brenda was dark-haired, dark-eyed, and tanned from the sun, they suspected that we were trying to smuggle a Mexican child across the border. After questioning her in Spanish, they realized that she was ours and returned her to me.

By now I had used up most of the money I had allocated for the trip, but in one of my phone calls home, Gene told me that he had been approved for SSI disability. It was a hard-fought battle to prove that his psychiatric disability interfered with his ability to hold down a job.

This meant the girls would retroactively be receiving benefits. Since we had never asked for or received money from Gene, the news was a new beginning for us. We decided to take the bus to San Francisco, because now I felt confident that whatever credit-card charges I would incur could easily be paid off.

The problem was that I had a credit card but no cash. Back in those days, many places would not accept a credit card. McDonald's being one. We had to eat in restaurants where we could charge our meals. This meant we had to bypass the fast-food places, which we preferred and could more easily afford.

One challenge after another.

We swam, we went sightseeing, and we laughed a lot. We felt normal. A heavy burden of despair was lifted.

It was a summer to remember and the perfect escape from Gene and all the baggage that he brought with him.

But we eventually had to come home.

TWENTY-SEVEN
The Thirteenth Step (late 1980s)

Gene's attempt at sobriety had so many tentacles. First, he had a feeling of grandiosity. In his manic state he decided that he was going to preach the gospel of sobriety. Because he had found his higher power, he thought that he must spread the word. He figured he would start small but would eventually become known the world over. He *knew* that he would eventually get his own TV show, like Billy Graham.

He rented a small hall and had his first and only meeting as an evangelist. Only five people showed up. Kenny Jackson and I were two. For us it was a command performance. I was there out of curiosity, and Kenny was there because he wanted to make sure that I would be okay.

Gene *was* going to AA meetings day and night. He turned all his energy into living the program. He was finally gaining the respect of the people in the rooms.

He read and interpreted the Big Book. He led Twelve Step meetings and was asked to speak at open meetings and anniversaries. All the energy he had put into causing harm was now focused on "Program."

Of course, he had to do some thirteen-stepping also. There are twelve steps to AA; the thirteenth step is not endorsed but is not uncommon.

Gene used AA as a hunting ground. Here he found vulnerable women and ignored the suggestion that the alcoholic avoid getting into a romantic relationship until at least one year of sobriety. Gene, however, started dating his "fellow" alcoholics very quickly.

In this environment he met Dorothy.

I met Dorothy when he brought her to my house under the guise of visiting with his now-adult daughters. I was caught off guard and invited them in. We went into the living room where he casually sat on the couch next to me. I was amazed when he draped his arm around my shoulder. I couldn't help but feel a tiny tinge of sympathy for her.

It wasn't long before they announced that they were going to get married. I thought that this was the best thing that could happen to me.

Although we were invited, the girls and I opted out of attending their wedding.

Dorothy was a woman of means, and I realized that Gene was not beyond being influenced by her bank account. Sure enough, after nine months of wedded bliss, she gave him a generous settlement to get out of the marriage.

Gene offered me a substantial amount of that money, in an effort to buy 10 Foster Place from me.

I agreed to sell it to him. I had been commuting fifty miles a day to and from work. I shared my house with Tina, who was by then married and had a son. We had talked about finding a two-family house closer to where I worked. This was, after all, the house where the murder took place and the house that was set on fire. There was no sentimental reason to hang on to this piece of real estate.

We settled on a financial agreement and again did a quick deed sale. I will say that Gene never missed a payment.

Tina found a two-family house that she loved, and it was five minutes from my school. We breathed deeply and applied for a mortgage.

The sale of the house gave Gene a way to channel his need for power and control. He now had a mission. He turned 10 Foster Place into a sober house. He rented four of the five bedrooms and the basement to men in recovery. He focused his need for control on them by demanding sobriety and attendance at AA meetings. The residents needed to do service at the meetings—make coffee, set up or clean up afterwards—and to get sponsors and read the Big Book. Somehow it worked.

During these years Gene touched many lives. Where he once was asked not to show up at certain church basements, he was gaining the respect of the people in the meeting rooms. His life was guided by the twelve steps and the Big Book of AA.

Although Gene had his short, doomed marriage to Dorothy and an on-again-off-again fling with another recovering alcoholic, he and I were still attached by what felt like an umbilical cord.

Oh, I admit I was angry. I did not want him. I did not need the drama and insanity. But why did I feel betrayed, hurt, and jealous? He had delivered me to the door of hell, and I feared that he was now going to live happily ever after. Without me!

When Gene explained to me that Dorothy might look a little older than her years because, and I quote, "*She* had a rough life," that was the last straw. Talk about irony.

It was time for me to move on.

TWENTY-EIGHT
Women in Distress (1992-1996)

My father had succumbed to cancer. I promised him that I would look after my mother. Although Gene was supportive during Dad's illness and was still committed to his sobriety, Mom did not trust him and was displeased that he kept popping into our lives. Her two sisters had relocated to southern Florida, and she made the decision to live near to them. She sold her home. Although it was hard for her leave her girls, she could now live far from Gene.

I was eligible to retire at fifty five, I had thirty-three years vested in the retirement system, and I was giving a lot of thought to where to go with my life. I knew that I was ready to leave teaching. I loved the work I was doing with prison families. I considered getting an advanced degree and pursuing a second career as a counselor, specializing in criminal justice. That way I could still do the work I loved, and I could continue to earn a living. My pension was not very much, and it would be seven years before I could apply for social security.

Sometime after Mom moved to Florida, my aunt passed away and left me a small inheritance. That and the money I was able to take out of my retirement fund was enough to buy a condo in the North Miami area of Florida. Now I could be near my mother. She was my strength.

My new home was a walk-up garden apartment in Co-
conut Creek, Florida, less than an hour from my mom's
house. Tina, her then husband, and my grandson Aaron
were settled into our New York home. Brenda was in a relationship with George, and Gene was remarried and living
in New York. I would now be able to concentrate on the rest
of my life.

Shirley and Abe were living in a gated senior community, also in south Florida. When their son was arrested while
living in California, they had reached out to the Fortune Society for information and support. They were directed to
our Hempstead Prison Families Anonymous group. They
became an integral part of our family for twenty years; Shirley always sure to bring her homemade brownies or donuts
to our meetings. Abe used his skills as a CPA to help us
with our bookkeeping. When Abe retired and they moved
to Florida, we remained in close touch. That's the way it was
with our families.

When I said I was moving to Florida, they were delight-
ed. However, Shirley and Abe wanted to make sure that I
had a cushion. They knew me well enough to know that I
would need a project, something to keep me busy. They did
their research and found an agency working with domestic violence survivors. Women in Distress was an all-in-one
agency, offering emergency shelter, a hotline, advocacy,
support groups, education, and prevention.

I went for an interview and was immediately "hired" as
a volunteer.

I participated in every aspect of Women in Distress,

accompanying women to court, helping them with paper-work, working the hotline, public speaking, and anything else that needed doing. The only thing I did not do was work in the thrift store, but I supported that by purchasing their wares.

By the end of year two, I was honored as Volunteer of the Year. Somewhere in their archives is a plaque with my name on it. I loved doing this; it allowed me to meet won-derful, like-minded folks.

Ellie Gorman was employed by Women in Distress. She and I became close friends. When she developed her own victim advocacy program in conjunction with the Lauder-hill Police Department, she asked me to come along with her as a victim advocate. I said yes.

This would be the other side of the coin. I accompanied the victims of crime to court proceedings, helped them fill out paperwork, advised them of their rights, and helped (I hoped) alleviate some of their trauma. Working with crime victims was a comfortable fit. I had always maintained that the families of the perpetrators were the unseen victims of crime.

JoAnne, an executive employee of Women in Distress, hooked me up with VISTA (Volunteers in Service to Amer-ica), and I represented Women in Distress as an advisor to the Broward Correctional Institution, a women's prison in Pembroke Pines, Florida. I had the opportunity to interact with the incarcerated women and their service providers. I learned much about the plight of women prisoners, some-thing that was to serve me well in later endeavors.

I knew the statistics. Most women in prison were there as a result of a drug crime, often being used as a mule to carry drugs for their men and therefore left to take the fall. It was also a fact that few men, other than their fathers, showed up on visiting days.

Sadly, I also learned that most of the women were mothers, whose children being cared for by grandparents or in the foster care system. All too often, these women lost custody of those children.

I also met women who were locked up because they fought back and were imprisoned because they killed their abusers. I looked at these women and realized that there was a fine line between them and me. I had a flashback to Gene, lying on the floor at my feet in a drunken stupor, with a gun to his head, and I thought how close I had come to kicking the hand holding the gun, with the thought that he would die and I would be so much better off.

Of course, I never acted on my instinct and so there I was as an observer and an advocate, wearing black instead of orange. I was quite content doing all of this when Art declared that we needed to start a PFA support group in southern Florida. And so we did.

Art arranged for us to have a room at the Jewish Community Center in Sunrise, Florida. Finding families to attend was easy.

I met Alice at a local Al-Anon meeting. She was visiting her alcoholic husband in a state prison and attending Al-Anon meetings to prepare her for his homecoming. Alice and I lived in the same community.

Val, who worked for my cousin as a domestic, was fighting to get out of an abusive marriage. I accompanied her to attorney meetings and family court. During all of this mayhem, her son was committing minor offenses, eventually leading to the event that earned him LWOP (Life Without Parole). Val is a strong woman who was not intimidated by the hand that she was dealt. She is now living a good life, remarried, helping to support her aging mother, and is an inspiration and role model to her grandchildren.

Jan, the divorced mother of four grown children, was married to Bill, a man who was in prison in Indiana. She met him through a pen pal request he had placed in a church bulletin. They corresponded, spoke on the phone a few times, and she fell in love. Jan would go to visit him once a year, until he came home and picked up on his old ways. Jan was also a volunteer at Women in Distress.

Shelley was referred by the Aleph Institute, an Orthodox organization that sees to the spiritual needs of Jewish prisoners. Her son was in an automobile accident that left him with a brain injury. As a result he acted inappropriately and was sent to prison as a sex offender. He had a terribly difficult time being in compliance with the institutional rules and was punished over and over for a condition over which he had no control. Shelley fought the good fight to have his conviction overturned, but the system showed no compassion (nor any common sense).

Through word of mouth, people found us and we had support group meetings every other week.

I procrastinated over registering at a college and never

fulfilled my ambition to continue on for an advanced degree that would enable me to get the credentials to open a practice. So there I sat with sixty credits above my bachelor's degree, years of practical experience, and no way to make a living.

Shortly after I moved into my Florida "dollhouse," Gene and Dorothy finalized their divorce. Their marriage had lasted all of nine months. Now he was free, clean, and sober, and only a long car ride away. I got a phone call that he was leaving New York and twenty-four hours later he was at my front door. I couldn't help it—I looked forward to his visit. Damn! I still cared so much and was tired of fighting the feelings.

He ingratiated himself with my new friends and neighbors. No one knew our history or had a clue about the secrets we carried. He helped me get my new home in order, putting up shelves, doing minor repairs, changing light fixtures, and making sure I had a well-stocked toolbox. We dined out, went to concerts, and he treated me well.

My mother cautioned me that a leopard cannot change his spots. Maybe not, but Gene was sober. All was right with the world. Years went by, mercifully uneventful.

Then my mother became ill. She had cancer. It was devastating. She lingered for a year. We hired a full-time caregiver for her, eventually relying on hospice. Gene was there for us, emotionally and practically. He accompanied us to doctor appointments, did minor repairs around her condo, and helped hold her up when she was too weak to stand on her own. He encouraged her to eat when she had no appetite and he told her not to worry about me. Maybe the leopard's spots were fading.

My mother was able to die without the fear of leaving me in the clutches of Gene, the monster. No matter what your age, you are never prepared to be an orphan.

Our children were living productive lives. Tina had joined the New York City Police Department. We watched proudly as her son, Aaron, had his bar mitzvah. Brenda was in a serious relationship with George, whom she eventually married.

Gene and I were left to define this new interaction. We were again traveling parallel paths that continually intersected. It was like a magnetic pull. I love you, I love you not.

TWENTY-NINE
Another Crisis (1997)

I was living my life, trying to find balance in what I was doing.

As a teacher I had my summer vacations to live my fantasies. Before I married I traveled internationally, seeing Europe on five dollars a day, enjoying the adventure of traveling by rail, hitching rides, sleeping on trains, and subsisting on bread and cheese.

Now, these many years later, I tried to pick up where I left off. I found my adrenalin could start pumping as much by the anticipation of a trip, say to Israel, as by the fear of a stalking spouse.

So travel I did, both domestically and overseas. I found the time to do it all—Prison Families Anonymous meetings, speaking engagements, and advocacy, both in Florida and New York.

There was always a feeling of sadness in my inner core, but I had the art of acting "as if" down to a science.

I was on a trip with my friends Ellie and Allyn. Our travels took us to Las Vegas with a side trip to Hoover Dam. Gene and I were in daily contact. I phoned Gene to let him know we were settling in for the night. After the usual "hello" and "what's new," he told me he was not feeling well.

"I've been pissing a lot of blood, Barb. It's been happening a lot and going on for a long time now," he said in one long breath.

"And the doctor said ...?"

"Well, he wants me to go for tests. I really don't know what to do. The test will be really intrusive, and it will hurt like hell."

At least he saw a doctor.

I knew that it was time for me to go back home—to New York, to Gene.

New York was always home to me. I had kept the house on Long Island and one or both of my daughters always kept the hearth warm for me.

It was winter when I arrived home. I found a phone message waiting for me.

"Hello, my name is Freddie Staller, and I am calling from the Long Island Community Foundation. I think we have a Christmas gift for you."

As it turned out the gift was a $1,000 grant designated for an organization on Long Island that was helping the families of prisoners. The money was funneled through the Long Island Community Foundation by a gentleman who had read a story about a child who had an incarcerated parent and felt motivated to help.

After contacting many criminal-justice agencies, the LICF found us. I met this generous donor and after we spoke, he increased his offer to $25,000. PFA, with the assistance of other organizations (Family and Children Services, Long Island Progressive Coalition, Federal Employment and Guidance Service) was able to expand its services.

PFA meetings had continued during my absence. Susan McCasland facilitated the meetings at a church in Deer Park. We had no money, no staff, no office, but we had a meeting room and people who needed each other.

THIRTY
Back to Jail (2000-2003)

With the incentive of revitalizing our program, I spoke with my friend Barbara Treen, a former Prison Families Anonymous board member and retired parole commissioner. We decided to work together again and restructure PFA. Since we had let our nonprofit status go dormant, we needed to go under the umbrella of one or another of these agencies, finally choosing Federation Employment and Guidance Service (FEGS) as our home base.

FEGS was an agency dedicated to human services, and they became our fiscal agent for a few years. During this time our membership and advocacy efforts increased. Barbara and I again established a relationship with the Nassau County Correctional Center where, with the help of volunteers, we set up a program in the visiting area of the jail.

There was no longer a cigarette vending machine. The building I had visited many years ago was in disrepair, although it was still used for reception and to house women. Where once there had been a productive farm and work-release facility, there was now a new building surrounded by barbed wire. This was where persons sentenced by the court to serve a year or less, or those awaiting disposition of their cases—being held without any bail or unable to make their bail—were housed.

Outside this building was a visiting trailer. It was in this uncomfortable setting that visitors began the process of visitation. There they showed their IDs and gave the name of the person they hoped to visit. If they were lucky—if the ID was current, if the inmate was not out at court or medical, or had not used up his or her allotted visits for the week—they were given a tag with a number and told to wait until their number was called. Just like a bakery. Sometimes they had to wait over an hour before being allowed into the main visiting room, where they turned in their IDs and were given a key to a locker in which to leave their belongings. They were not allowed to bring jewelry, keys, hair pins, money, or anything that might set off the metal detectors (and that included the underwire in a bra) into the actual visiting area.

It was in the trailer that Barbara and I set up the operation we called "The Beacon." We were there to offer support, caring, and cookies—and information on how to negotiate the intimidating system. We offered families hope, strength, and a safe place to land. We told them how to find food banks, attorneys, bail, victims' assistance, and anything else they might need.

To accomplish this we published a pamphlet that explained the rules and regulations of the county jail, with a glossary of pertinent terms. Many people did not know the difference between a jail and a prison. What is an arraignment? What is a misdemeanor or a felony? It was Criminal Justice 101. We called it, appropriately, *The Visitor's Handbook.*

It also contained information about the state prison system. Many county inmates sit in jail for months, or even years waiting for trial or to be offered a plea. The lucky ones are out on bail, but the unfortunate ones who cannot afford to post bail sit there just waiting. Only people who have been sentenced to county time (a year or less) are allowed to work on the grunge jobs that keep the jails functioning. Once their case is adjudicated, they are sent into unknown terrain. They now belong to the state.

Sing Sing is no longer a reception area. A new prison was built, Downstate Correctional Facility, initially as a pre-release facility, but it opened as a reception center. New prisons were being built all over the state. We were up to more than seventy prisons during this era. If you build them, you need to fill them.

So began the era of mass incarceration.

While the balloon was inflating, we were trying to decompress the anxiety of those who were the recipients of the new waves of arrests.

Some of the volunteers who sat in the trailer were community people. Some were my former teaching colleagues, but most were prison families.

Sometimes lives intersect. Back in 1959, Lois and I explored Europe together as two curious, somewhat naive young adults. Now we sat together, two retired school teachers, in the visiting area of a jail.

We tried to humanize a system that thrived on conformity and blandness. When visitors walked into our trailer, they required a few seconds to realize they were in a jail extension and not a first grade classroom. Lois, who taught kindergarten, and Marge, a retired grade teacher, brought all levels of age-appropriate reading books, coloring books, and crayons for the children. We could see their eyes light up when they were given these gifts and their pride when they saw their finished art taped to the wall.

We were able to introduce a few more positive changes. At our prodding, the jail administration put a clock in the visiting area and installed a pay phone and soda machine at the entrance to the trailer (this was before the days when everyone had a cell phone). After months of unrelenting advocacy, working with the NAACP and other advocates, we saw Saturday visits reinstated at the jail.

We held mini-counseling sessions as we sat among the visitors, drying tears, dispelling fears, and acting as peacemakers between the visitors and the correction officers. There is a natural distrust between the keepers and the kept, which spills over to the visitors. Our PFA volunteers bridged that gap somewhat. We acted as a buffer between correction officers and a sometimes frustrated, sometimes angry visitor.

A visitor to the jail had to abide by many rules, some of which seemed unreasonable to them. We were able to explain the reasons for the procedures and act as a calming influence.

There were many feel-good stories.

We were able to arrange a visit for a woman who had an expired ID. She suffered from multiple sclerosis and needed a cane to assist her in walking. She had moved to Florida and returned to Long Island when she heard that her only child had been arrested here. She was staying with a former neighbor for two weeks, hoping to see her son as often as possible. Her visit had been denied because her ID had just expired, although it had been accepted by the airline. She had a Medicare card, an MS ID card, and voter registration card, but they told her she could not visit. We intervened, and she was able to visit at all appropriate times during her stay.

We encouraged visitors to assist each other by sharing rides and translating for each other.

A three-year-old girl who was there to visit her father regularly brought me a handful of flowers (weeds) and hugged me hello and goodbye.

There was a fourteen-year-old boy who always looked sullen. He did not want to be there, but his father insisted that he come and visit his older brother. One day I asked him if he might help me by going around with the cookies so I could speak with a distressed visitor. My manipulation worked. He eventually came in and picked up the tin of candy without being asked and made the rounds of the trailer with a smile on his face.

We consoled a six-year-old who was crying uncontrollably because her daddy had already had his allotment of three visits, which meant she was unable to see him. Mom was on the verge of tears herself. A lollipop and a hug helped them both.

There was the very pregnant woman who had a wired bra and was told to either take it off or not have a visit. She took her bra off, left it with me, and with arms crossed over her breasts walked through the metal detector and visited her husband.

A trail of distressed people kept coming and going, wet from waiting in the rain for the trailer to open its doors, freezing in the winter, and sweating in the summer.

We have witnessed weddings, and we have been there to offer consolation to people who have suffered a loss.

Bringing candy, cookies, or lollipops is no longer allowed. Someone might choke and sue the jail.

Corrections did away with the trailer. Visitors now stand in a queue in the parking lot, waiting in rain, snow, heat, with baby carriages or canes. But there is no need for extra officers or extra compassion.

My professional involvement with the Nassau County Correctional Center was pretty much coming to an end. We had started our outreach program at the jail back in 1976, where we did crisis intervention, referrals, and family advocacy. The following year we developed a training program for correction officers with the goal of sensitizing the staff to the needs of the families.

In 1978 we collaborated with the staff to develop a *Visitors' Regulation Book* and in the late 1980s, with the help of Touro Law Center, we updated it and printed *The Visitors' Handbook*.

Under the current administration, we no longer have a place in the jail, and all weekend visitation has been discontinued.

Our only ongoing involvement with the jail has been to

go into the visiting lobby the week before Christmas with toys for the children who are visiting. We accept donations of unwrapped, brand-new toys, which we put on display in the lobby. The children are allowed to pick a toy or more than one if it was a good year for donations. If the children are young enough to believe us, we tell them the toy was given to us, for them, by their daddy, mommy, brother, or whoever they are there to visit.

This has been a tradition for close to thirty-five years. Administrations changed, sheriffs came and went, and the work-release facility was turned into a menacing barbed wire-surrounded structure. But every December PFA was there, somewhere, in the visiting area, with our bags of toys and boxes of tissues for the running noses and to wipe away the tears.

During many of those years we partnered on this project with Bobby Moore, the administrator of the drug and alcohol tier at the jail. Bobby was an ex-con and an addict who, while still in prison, chose Kenny Jackson as his sponsor. He worked his way from a suicidal, depressed drunk to a person who was respected by many people in the recovery community.

When Kenny gave up running the therapeutic Fortune tier at the jail, he bequeathed it to Bobby, and it was re-named the Drug Alcohol Rehabilitation Treatment (DART) program. Bobby became our champion, helping us find new benefactors, transporting the toys, and supplying lists of families we needed to visit, with or without our reindeer.

Unfortunately, recovery was a slippery slope for Bobby,

and he died much too young.

Some families were physically unable to go to the jail to visit. Perhaps the child's mother was a codefendant, or had an outstanding warrant, or no valid ID. That did not matter to us because if there was a child at home and Christmas was approaching, we were going to get the gifts to them.

Going into some neighborhoods meant scooting past the drug dealers and pimps hanging out on the front porches. I was always treated with respect, had doors held open, and heavy packages carried into the buildings for me. I was recognized as the lady who helps us in the jail. I never felt threatened.

Ron Wood would come to the jail with bushels of toys from the Society of Saint Vincent de Paul, where he worked at the time. Churches would donate, and we always had more elves than we needed for organizing and volunteering.

So far none of the administrators has placed obstacles in our way. Some sheriffs and staff welcomed us and some ignored us.

One of the staff who welcomed us was Regina Lee, another of my sheroes. Regina was a social worker at the jail and was always a champion for those in her care. After Bobby died, she became our go-to person at the jail. She made the calls to ensure that we would be welcomed back with our toys and that we would have the continued support of the jail staff. Not all the officers in the visiting area were happy to see us, but Regina was always able to smooth things out.

She is our stern but loving elf, using her organizational skills in arranging the toys, making sure we always have something to eat or drink and enough toilet paper in the women's bathroom.

Our last year might have been 2017. We'll see. I hope the tradition will be carried on by others. If I decide not to go back, or if the jail administration discontinues our toy give-away, my memory will always hold a collage of little smiling faces looking up with amazement when we say, "These toys are here for you."

Since her retirement, Regina has accepted a position on the Board of Directors of PFA; she has helped us tremendously, particularly with fund raising. She has joined us at presentations and represents us on the Nassau County Re-entry Task Force.

With the discontinuation of weekend visits, PFA has again joined with advocates questioning the policies of the local jail.

THIRTY-ONE
'Til Death Do Us Part (1997-1999)

After twenty years of not drinking, Gene was dying. He had always promised me he was going to die young. I never believed it. I was sure he would outlive me. Didn't I read somewhere that only the good die young?

We visited doctors, proctologists, urologists, and oncologists. They all said the same thing—bladder cancer. They might be able to treat it, although the treatment would be invasive, and he needed to stop smoking immediately.

Gene was a chain smoker. Every shirt he owned had to have a breast pocket to hold a pack of cigarettes. As it was with his drinking, he was told the consequences, continued the destructive behavior, and refused the prescribed treatment.

Instead, he quadrupled the vitamins he was taking. Dr. Jekyll got out his blender and mixed and matched the whole alphabet of vitamins, minerals, antioxidants, and whatever the cure of the day might be. He even convinced me to increase my intake.

"Barbara, it might be too late for me, but we can avoid this happening to you."

He became obsessed with my health and with finding the organic cure for cancer. He would have vitamins sent to me from mail-order stores, the same stores that I used when I sent vitamins to Green Haven.

In my cynicism I could not help but wonder about his concern for me. Who would care for him if I was not okay? Control? Love? I chose to believe those vitamins were the equivalent of the bouquets of flowers he used to bring me during the good times. When we were first married and Gene was working in Manhattan, he commuted by way of the Long Island Railroad. Every Friday, his payday, he would buy a bouquet of flowers at Penn Station, carry it with him for the hour-long train ride, and walk in the door with a smile and a hug.

"Listen to the urologist. Try the treatment. It's your life!" I implored.

"No, I don't have to. Statistically speaking, I still have five to ten years. Once you're diagnosed, it doesn't mean you die right away."

He needed to believe this. Gene was afraid to die. A small part of him feared that there was a heaven and a hell. Where did the universe send men who killed their fathers?

The pain medication he was prescribed did not help. He added marijuana. It did relieve the pain, but his mood swings returned. One day he would hold me, and we would cry in each other's arms as he begged me to remarry him. He would plan for our future, as if he really thought we would have a lifetime together. My heart would break over and over. I knew that there would be no future for us, even if he should miraculously survive.

Then his mood would switch. He would turn from a gentle, loving man into someone who was acting irrationally, yelling that I did not care what happened to him and that I was putting him in the hospital to get rid of him. Besides, if he was in the hospital, he could not smoke, and there I went, trying to control him again.

The medical staff assumed that Gene and I were married. I had never changed my name back to my maiden name, and no one ever asked. I was allowed access to all medical information, and I was given a voice in decision-making. Gene encouraged me to be with him during each phase of his treatment. I sat with him during exams, treatments, and evaluations. I never for a moment considered walking away. His vulnerability grabbed at my heartstrings; as always, my emotions took precedence over rational thought. Gene needed me, so where else would I be?

I was not able to physically (or psychologically) care for Gene. Although the people he met in the rooms of AA and those he sheltered in the house on Foster Place showed their concern and compassion by assisting in his care, all the decision-making and actual caregiving became my responsibility. There was no one else. After his last hospitalization, I decided to hire a caregiver. That lightened my burden and allowed me to step back a little.

I was regressing into the world I thought I had left behind long ago. My thoughts and deeds focused only on Gene. I was not taking care of my own needs. I couldn't sleep. I jumped at the slightest unexpected sound. I was binge-eating, and I was having nightmares. Déjà vu.

My children were now adults, and they were there beside me every step of the way, not questioning my decisions, helping by not judging us.

Only a few days after I hired a caregiver, the girls and I requested hospice. One of the requirements for hospice care was to sign a Do Not Resuscitate (DNR) order. Gene objected, but no one wanted him to suffer a lingering death. I had watched my father die of cancer; before he succumbed, he suffered excruciating pain. Hospice would not step in without a DNR, so eventually I signed it for him, and hospice took over Gene's care. By then he was drifting in and out of consciousness; he was not aware enough to object.

That decision carried some guilt. Even though I knew hospice was in his best interest, it was something he did not want. I felt uncomfortable. After all, I had spent most of my adult life trying to please Gene.

Hospice sent nurses, a doctor, and a social worker. They cared for him and comforted me, even after I confessed that I was divorced from Gene.

'Til death do us part.

Three days after I approved hospice—with Tina, Brenda, and me at his bedside—Gene used his last breath to whisper, "Barbara, help me." And then he died, releasing his grip on me for the very last time.

Gene was gone but my work was far from over.

THIRTY-TWO
Lifers (circa 2000)

Different sentences are imposed when people are found guilty of a crime. They can be given a flat sentence, in which case the inmate knows the release date. They can be sentenced to five, ten, or twenty years, at which time they will be released, perhaps with post-release supervision. They can earn merit time, which shows that they behaved, took all mandated programs, and seldom got into trouble. This might mean being released six months early.

Gene got an indeterminate sentence, with a maximum date of seven years, but he was eligible for release after completing his minimum time. In his case the two-and-a-half years came with "good time" up front, so he got out after only two years, an extraordinary sentence even then.

An indeterminate sentence is not used as much anymore, except in cases of a "violent felony offender" conviction. Most of those sentences have life at the end. These are the folks who go to the parole board over and over again and are told to come back for reappearance in two years.

Then we have a sentence known as LWOP, Life Without Parole.

The last two categories make up the population known as lifers.

Years after Gene was released from prison, Prison Families Anonymous was invited to meet with the lifers group at Sing Sing. My friend and colleague Barbara Treen and I drove up to Ossining, New York, and I found myself back in the parking lot with that same hill and that overpowering gun tower. This time I was without packages or children, but the old tapes started playing and I felt a little shiver. We were processed in, and the guard led us into a room somewhere in the bowels of the prison. We were greeted by a group of men who were serving life sentences. I always felt more comfortable with the men in their green uniforms than I did with the correction officers (COs). I knew that the people who invited us were pleased that we were there while the COs thought of us as a nuisance.

Although our hosts were aware that there was a possibility they might never be released from prison, these men wanted to explore options and stimulate their curiosity. They needed to be part of a world outside of their immediate environment. Most felt a sense of remorse and wanted to give something back to society, rather than slowly waste away. They published a newsletter to share, not only with their fellow inmates but also mailed out to civilians.

Barbara and I were happy to be invited and hoped that our visit would serve as a link to the outside world for these men. My reason for going inside the walls was to allow the men the opportunity to address thoughts and feelings about the people they left behind. Often their issues with families become exaggerated and distorted when seen through the prism of steel bars and mesh wires.

We brought a video with us and needed an outlet to plug

in the power cord. Then we were told that just on the other side of the door was the room that once held the electric chair. We were currently in a room that was known as the dance hall. The last few hours of the convicted person's life were spent in this room as he or she waited to "be seated." Music was piped into the room to soothe the person about to be electrocuted. Thus the name—the dance hall.

There were plenty of outlets in that room. But by then the electric chair, fondly known as Old Sparky, had been moved to Green Haven.

It was an eerie feeling.

I was invited to meet with the lifers at Shawangunk, another maximum-security prison in downstate New York. Frankie, whose mother Connie was an advocate and a regular at Prison Families Anonymous support groups, was a lifer currently doing his time there.

It was a last minute invite, but I thought that it would be a worthwhile gig so I gathered a bunch of our brochures, hoping to distribute them. They described the services provided by PFA, and contained our contact information. One of the reasons for going into prisons was to encourage the residents to have their families reach out to us.

While being processed, I showed my stack of brochures to the CO and was told that I would not be allowed to bring them in. I would have needed to send it to the prison prior to my visit so that it could be checked for contraband. That was no problem. I walked in empty handed, with no prepared speech, but certainly with an idea of what I planned to say.

Everything went well. Our hosts, the lifers, provided us with food and beverages. The door to the yard was left open so we could intermingle until we, the guests, were called to make our brief presentations. I stuck to my topic and was well received. After the presentation, many of the men individually asked me how their families could contact PFA. I suggested they call our cyberspace telephone number, which they wrote down. We did not have an office, since we were an organization of volunteers without funding at that time. Many men wrote down the official PFA number.

A correction officer approached and said that I was giving out my phone number "a lot." I replied with a smile that I had not given my phone number out that much since I was sixteen years old. Ha, ha.

Apparently someone was offended because weeks later I received a letter from the powers that be saying that I was not welcome back at Shawangunk Correctional Facility. (By then the prisons were no longer called "prisons." The names have changed but not so much the mission.) The letter was thoughtful enough to explain the reason: I gave out *my* phone number, and they actually quoted my comment. I always knew my sense of humor could get me in trouble. And so, as the femme fatale of the geriatric generation, I was denied admittance to a prison. It is easier to get out than it is to get in.

A year or two later, I cosponsored a conference with the National Community Sentencing Association. There were many dignitaries attending the conference, some from the Department of Corrections, and I told the Shawangunk tale from the podium. It drew a few laughs and an invitation for me to go back anytime I chose. I never did find an occasion alluring enough to entice me back.

THIRTY-THREE
New Yorkers Against the Death Penalty
(circa 2000)

I have always been an opponent of the death penalty. I could not understand the rationale for killing people. I knew from common sense and from the information learned in the Sociology101 class I took at Hofstra that the death penalty serves no purpose other than revenge. It is not a deterrent to murder. People who kill do not think before doing the dastardly deed, "Gee, I better not do this, or I might get the death penalty."

I read in the upcoming events section of the newspaper that there was going to be a symposium at St. John's University. The topic: The Death Penalty. The scheduled speaker would be David Kaczynski, the director of New Yorkers Against the Death Penalty (NYADP). David was the brother of Ted Kaczynski, the infamous Unabomber.

I, along with most people of my age, had a vivid recollection of the capture of the Unabomber and the details that led up to it. David was one of my heroes.

Accompanying David and sharing the stage would be family members of murdered victims. They would be telling stories of horrendous loss. I could only think how brave and unique they must be. It seemed important that some of us, who loved the perpetrators of violent crimes, listen to the voices of the victims. Roz, Betty, and Ida agreed to go with me.

I had once been asked to speak on a panel with survivors. When I arrived at the venue, I was informed by the organizer of the event that the other panelists had refused to appear with anyone who represented families of killers. Of course, I chose to walk away. I totally understood their position. I am not sure how I would react if someone hurt my child or grandchild. Personally, I might want to exact revenge, but I do know that I would not want the state to kill the killer—unless that would bring my loved one back.

I was listening to these brave people express their concerns that after their loved ones' killers were apprehended, the state intended to execute them. They objected to this.

"Why do we kill people to show people that killing people is wrong?"

The first speaker told a harrowing story that I will not soon forget. He, let's call him Bill, was with his wife when the perps came in to rob their store. Shots were fired, and both were hit by bullets. His wife was mortally wounded, but he survived his injuries and described how he held his wife in his arms as he watched her die, not sure if he was going to bleed to death before help arrived.

Bill traveled the NYADP circuit to reiterate that he did not want to see the killers murdered in the name of his wife.

David told the story of how he found out that his brother was culpable in the deaths and wounding of innocent people and the struggle that he and his wife, Linda, went through before they made the inevitable decision to go to the authorities with what they knew about Ted.

Most heart-wrenching was his telling of how he broke the news to his mother. David is a tall man, and his mother is a very petite woman. As he told his mother that her son, his brother, was a serial killer and that he, David, needed to report him to the authorities, this wise woman raised her hands to embrace David's face; instead of berating him, she commiserated with how difficult the decision must have been for him. It took forbearance, but eventually David negotiated with the FBI and other authorities to spare his mentally ill brother the death penalty.

I had to suppress the urge to run up onto the stage and hug all of them. Instead, I patiently waited until the question-and-answer period, then raised my hand and introduced David and the panelists to Prison Families Anonymous. I was shaking a little and my voice quavered, fearful that we would be confronted with the same negative reaction I had encountered in the past. I did not want to place anyone in a position of discomfort. Of course, since I was the one who suggested that we attend, I felt entirely responsible for everyone's feelings. No need for me to have worried.

There was so much positive energy in that room!

Ida and Roz had sons who would be spending from twenty years to life in prison for taking lives. Here they were, deep in conversation with their counterparts, men and women whose loved ones had been victims of homicide. There were many shared emotions. All of us had suffered the loss of a loved one because of violence. Everyone here felt the futility—a moment of madness leading to the forever shattering of lives.

We all understood that the PFA families could still visit and communicate with the perpetrator. The survivors could only visit a grave site.

Eventually I accepted an invitation to be on the board of directors of NYADP. I was fortunate in that I was able to join with so many exceptional people in the fight to eliminate the death penalty. My old friend Jonathan Gradess, who had helped PFA with its incorporation, was a board member.

This work brought two sheroes into my life, women whom I will always consider friends: Marie Verzulli, the victim survivor advocate at NYADP, and Colleen Eren, the organizing director.

Colleen is a true warrior—young, slightly built, athletic, attractive, PhD, who recently authored *The Crisis of Bernie Madoff*. I have hope that the future will be secure if left in the able hands of the Colleens of this world.

Marie, a vibrant and upbeat woman, was never without a smile. How shocked I was to learn the reason for Marie's passion for justice. Years before I met Marie, there was a tragic event in upstate New York. A person was arrested as a serial killer. He murdered women he perceived to be prostitutes. By the time he was arrested he had a myriad of bodies rotting in his attic.

One of these unfortunate women was the sister of my new friend Marie. Despite the severity of the crime, Marie and her mother did not want the perpetrator to be sent to the death chamber by the state of New York. Instead, Marie channeled her energy into working toward the abolition of the death penalty. I was in awe of this brave woman.

One of Marie's more pleasurable responsibilities was to accompany exonerees around the state as they told their stories of injustice—prosecutorial misconduct, poor or non-existent legal counsel, and the many other minefields that face the accused. One of the people Marie traveled with was Greg Wilhoit. They were on the speaking circuit in down-state New York, and knowing the finances of NYADP, I suggested they stay with me rather than incur the expense of hotel rooms. To be honest, I looked forward to being in their company and felt privileged to be able to host these two remarkable people.

Greg was another role model. He survived five years in an Oklahoma prison, in solitary confinement on death row. He did not display anger or bitterness, but he was vehement that his story be told. And it was told, both by him and, along with the story of Ron Williamson, in John Grisham's non-fiction book, *The Innocent Man.*

Greg also allowed my friend Lori G to interview him for her cable TV show *The Hidden Truth*. Greg's story resonated with Lori because she believed that her husband was wrongfully convicted. He had already spent eighteen years in a New York prison, where he would die just a few short years later without being able to prove his innocence. The interview took place in my living room.

The days I spent with Greg and Marie were precious. There was a lot of laughing and camaraderie, but never did they lose sight of the *why* of their mission.

Each year in the United States there are a significant number of exonerations. The number has been steadily rising, with 166 in 2016, according to statistics from the National Registry of Exonerations. These individuals are exonerated and released from prison, some from death row, often because DNA evidence proves their innocence and occasionally even exposes the guilty.

Such was the case with Jeffrey Deskovic. I was introduced to Jeffrey by Colleen.

There was an NYADP event at a local college. Colleen was accompanying Jeffrey, who was to be the keynote speaker.

His story encapsulated many that were similar. Jeffrey was a sixteen-year-old high school student in Westchester County, New York, when a young classmate was raped and murdered. Jeffrey was a quiet, introverted young man; because he was considered an outsider and not engaged in the usual teen activities, fingers pointed at him and he was soon brought to the attention of the police.

They brought this child into the precinct and relentlessly questioned him. He did not ask for a lawyer or a parent to be present, went hours without sleep, and was lied to and manipulated until finally he confessed to the crime.

Jeffrey spent sixteen years locked away in New York prisons. He knew that with the advances in testing of DNA evidence, it could finally be proven that his was a wrongful conviction. With the support of Barry Scheck and the Innocence Project, one would assume that this would just be a matter of protocol. And it would have been except for one barrier. Jeanine Pirro, who was the district attorney of Westchester County at the time, she of television fame, refused to allow Jeffrey's DNA to be tested. Whatever her motive or thought process, she held firm in her belief that Jeffrey was where he belonged. The county would not absorb the cost of testing this young man's DNA. Perhaps she really believed that her staff was infallible, and so Jeffrey had to be guilty.

Luckily for the good guys, Pirro was called to greener pastures, acting as a guest expert on all the TV crime and justice programs. Now real justice could happen. Westchester got a new district attorney, Jeffrey's DNA was tested, and it proved that it would not have been possible for him to have raped the poor child. But behold! There was a match. The real perp was identified, and justice was served. But not before this nonviolent young man served sixteen years in the bowels of hell for a crime he did not commit.

Jeffrey was released, without even a "sorry" from those who persecuted and prosecuted him, totally ill-prepared to function in the world he left behind. Yes, Jeffrey was awarded a large sum of money from the county and the state. He is using his award to try to help other wrongfully convicted people, but you cannot buy back sixteen years of a person's life.

By surrounding himself with other exonerees and advocates, staying positive, and focusing on his goals, Jeffrey is now attending law school

As my dear friend and colleague Dr. Eleanor Smith said

some twenty-five years earlier, "Execute justice, not people." At the present time, New York is not in the business of killing people.

In the hopes that this will be permanent, New Yorkers against the Death Penalty changed its name to New Yorkers for Alternatives to the Death Penalty. David Kaczynski retired and moved to a place where he and Linda can live the peaceful life they earned.

Recently, it was decided that our goal of no longer using state-sanctioned killing was accomplished and NYADP was able to close its doors.

The United States of America has not caught up with the rest of the civilized world. There are still some states that continue to allow the use of the death penalty, despite the increasing number of wrongful convictions.

THIRTY-FOUR
Women in Prison (2001)

I met Serena while she was incarcerated in Bedford Hills Correctional Facility in New York State. Barbara Treen was driving up to visit a woman for whom she was advocating. She suggested that I travel with her and visit with Serena, a fellow Long Islander. Coincidentally, although I had never met him, Serena's father had called me a time or two after "the incident."

While waiting in the visiting room, I looked around and noted how few men were visiting. It reminded me of the time I served on the advisory of the Broward Prison for Women.

Whatever prison I visit, the rooms are filled with women—female friends, mothers, wives, grandmothers, and sisters make up the volume of visitors. Fathers, brothers, and sons are in the minority, even at our support group meetings.

Unfortunately, this does not shock me. Women are the nurturers, the caregivers. I'm busy analyzing, thinking that most of these women are in prison because they were influenced by a husband or boyfriend.

"You can carry the drugs [be the mule]."

"Shit, if you get caught, they go easy on girls."

"If you love me, you will carry the gun [drive the car, or give me an alibi]."

Am I being sexist? Maybe.

These thoughts ran through my head as I sat in the visiting room, waiting. The longer I waited, the more nervous I became. No matter how many jails and prisons I visit in my lifetime, I will never get over the anxiety. I still jump at the sound of the clanging gates. I need to take deep breaths and meditate a few minutes before I encounter the scrutiny and the underlying tension that is behind every wall and barbed wire fence.

Finally, Serena approached me. I am sure she was confused as to why this stranger was visiting her. Who was this "elderly" woman, and what was she doing here?

She was no more confused than I was. I knew the reason for her conviction, a domestic tragedy that she could not avoid, but the facts of her crime be damned. I saw a very young, vulnerable-looking woman with a big smile. She was attractive, even in her prison garb, younger than my youngest daughter. She was bright, verbal, and had a wonderfully positive attitude. She looked as out of place in prison as Tina would have.

I barely remember the conversation, but the time went quickly; when our visit ended, I knew I would be back. I am sure I asked her how she was surviving behind the walls and what her plans were upon her release. I told her a little about myself and explained that I was there because of my friendship with Barbara, who was just a table away from us, absorbed in conversation with her client, Catherine. Although cross-visiting was not allowed, we were able to bend the rules slightly and acknowledge each other.

I knew that Serena would be staying in my life. It was hard for me to walk out and leave her sitting there.

That never changes, the pain of leaving someone behind.

Sure enough, I visited Serena as often as I was able. When she was released, I stayed in touch and watched her grow into an independent person who worked her way from prisoner to a highly respected professional, a role model and an advocate for the voiceless. Most important to her is her role as a wife to Gregory and mother to James.

I would be proud to think that I helped her navigate the world of reentry and beyond. However, Serena had the inner fortitude and a passion that served her well. She just needed little help from outside sources.

Elaine Lord was the warden at Bedford Hills during this time. She was forward-thinking and believed that the women in her care were deserving of compassion and should be given the tools needed for a productive return to society. Sister Elaine Roulet served as chaplain, spiritual advisor, and angel to the women at Bedford Hills. The two Elaines formed a powerful bond and together established model programs designed to assure that the women in their institution would be prepared for their eventual release and not just be warehoused. This was almost unheard of in the culture of American prisons.

These two women understood that most incarcerated women were mothers of children and that few of them would be receiving Mother of the Year awards. While living on the outside, these mothers might have neglected their children. With a little help and in the light of sobriety, their maternal instincts could be revitalized. It was essential to address parenting issues. For example, they established a nursery in the prison for women who gave birth there, allowing for mother and child to bond during the critical first year of the child's life.

They encouraged visitation by inviting outside agencies to transport children to the facility and enlisted the residents of the community of Bedford Hills to serve as hosts to the children, so that they could spend additional time with their mothers. To assure that the visits were nurturing, parenting classes were incorporated into the programming. The actual visits took place in the newly opened Children's Center. This was an area set aside so that children and their moms could make the most of their time together. Much thought was given to how best to utilize the space to benefit the population. A bright, cheery room filled with toys and books and lots of love was the answer.

Statistically, children who have an incarcerated parent have a better than average chance of winding up in prison.

Too many women housed in prisons are victims of domestic violence. This was another issue that needed to be addressed, and the administration at the Bedford Hills facility again encouraged outsiders with expertise to come behind the walls and work with the women, many of whom were incarcerated because they took extreme actions to break free of their abusers.

There but for fortune went I. How easily it could have been me wearing prison greens. One more slap from Gene, one more threat—could I have been the one to pick up a weapon and try to defend myself? I think not, but I imagine that most of the women inside thought the same thing.

As we prepared for another trip to Bedford Hills, Barbara Treen mentioned that there was a lady—and I use this term deliberately— who fit this profile. She had been incarcerated for almost twenty years. She was also a neighbor of ours on Long Island. Although Marie had a supportive family and was seldom left out on visiting days, Barbara thought it might be nice if we included her in our visits. A friend of mine, Helen, who worked at the Office of Women's Services in Suffolk County, enthusiastically agreed to join us and visit Marie. Our circle was growing.

Marie won her freedom after serving more than twenty years, thanks to the efforts of her son, who became an attorney with the goal of seeking justice for his mother. Their story could be a Lifetime movie, but Marie keeps a low profile and lives for her gardening, cooking, and her grandchildren. She is a proud, elegant, and independent woman, and I am proud to call her my friend.

THIRTY-FIVE
Fifty Years Later (2015-2017)

Although Gene has been gone many years, I continue my journey for justice. It has been a long one, and I have met so many people along the way. Each person deserves a chapter, some a book of his or her own. Some do have books of their own.

Every time I thought about stepping back a bit, another tentacle drew me in. Of course it was always about the families. Each new call from someone in pain convinces me that I can't leave, not yet. And beyond that there continues to be a pull towards issues of justice.

Fifty years have gone by and Prison Families Anonymous is still functioning, though not as vigorously. We are once again without a funding base, but we are still needed. As I get into my octogenarian years, I do so with a sense of sadness. I have lived to see the cycles and watched as the system swallowed itself and grew us into an era of mass incarceration, where punishment, revenge, and a lack of humanity is the norm.

People continue to feel that agonizing pain when the phone rings and the voice on the other end says, "This is Jane. I am in jail. Will you meet me at arraignment court with bail money?"

Or the operator says, "This is a collect call from a correctional facility. Will you accept the charges?"

Or when the date is nearing for the parole hearing and this is his third appearance. He was denied twice before because of the "nature of the crime," and you know that is something that will never change. You hope but don't expect.

Or you hear that he is in "the box" or has been transferred to a prison eight hours away.

Or worse still, you haven't heard from him in weeks; when you call the prison, they will not give you any information. Is he in the hospital, the box, angry at me for something I did or did not do? I can't fix this if I don't know what's wrong.

The reality is that the system is so broken that there is not much I can fix, even with knowledge and desire.

Sometimes, we are told that she is coming home but has few prospects for housing or a job. I guess she will have to come live with us, although she is thirty years old and is returning as almost a stranger. The alternative is a homeless shelter, and we know that they are unsafe, mostly drug filled, and empty of services. The residents are usually told they need to be out all day, supposedly looking for jobs. Not an easy task when you have few skills, no go-to-an-interview clothing, and little self-esteem.

All parolees are required to go to anger management and drug treatment—even if they never had a drug problem. Or they may have been in prison for twenty-five years and have taken the same drug program numerous times. It is difficult to hold down a job if your program conflicts with your work hours.

The parole officer usually holds back permission to drive. The family may live where public transportation is daunting. So many of our parolees need to beg a ride, or bicycle to work, in rain, sleet, or snow.

If we ever reform the reformatory system, we here on Long Island should work on the transportation system.

When I think that I am tired and it is time to walk away, I think about Danny. He did his time with no infractions and came home to his family determined to do all the right things as he faced five years of post-release supervision. He went to his assigned programs, never stayed out past curfew, and always had clean urine. He was the ideal parolee.

Danny was offered a union job, with good pay and a chance for advancement. Not many companies will hire a convicted felon. Danny knew he was lucky, and he was excited to be offered a job where they knew about his past and were still willing to hire him.

Danny followed protocol and told his parole officer about this great opportunity.

Perfect. Here was a real success story. A felon had changed his life and was taking steps to become an upstanding taxpaying citizen. There was going to be one less person out there without prospects. Of course, the parole officer would put out his hand and offer Danny congratulations,

You think?

Hell no! The job would keep the parolee out after curfew, and it was in New York City, out of the county. Permission denied.

Danny did not go back to drugs or crime. He finished his five years of post-release supervision, but he now has to start his career search over again. Instead of helping, parole just put up another barrier.

Of course, I may I get a call that Dennis is using again. Or the parole officer may give him a violation for missing curfew or not showing up for something or other.

Here's another one. Kenneth reported to parole with a box cutter on his person. He used it for his job, stocking shelves, and he went to parole right from work. He did not commit a crime with it or threaten anyone. He did not even try to hide it. The box he cut with it did not bleed or file a complaint. The parole officer did not give him a warning. There are no second chances. That work tool got him a violation and a year in the county jail.

What shall we do? To whom can we talk? That's when the phone rings at PFA. We no longer have an office, but the phone is still active.

Sue or Linda might pick up the call. They might not have a solution but they might have some of the answers. More important, they listen and they empathize. We know that listening helps, but it is not always enough. Sue might call a chaplain in the jail. We are grateful to the chaplains in our county jails. It does not matter the ethnicity or religion, or lack thereof, our chaplains will walk into a housing unit with a smile, some encouragement, and a watchful eye.

What a relief for Jo when Sue tells her that Sister Michelle or Deacon Jose has seen her son and he is fine.

The caller might be given the phone number for the watch commander, told to call the inmate's counselor, or whom to contact in Medical. We might give them the phone number for a van service that drives to Attica or the phone number of another family who might be willing to car pool.

We encourage our families to make the calls themselves. If the incarcerated person can write a letter or put in for an appeal, they need to be encouraged to do it for themselves.

We know about retaliation so when necessary, we will be the "beard" and complain on their behalf.

But always, the callers are encouraged to come to a meeting, because whatever their problems, there are those among us who have had them too.

Linda and Shirley, John and Jackie, Ida, and so many others are living proof that we do survive, despite the worry, the stress, the long drives, the trailer visits, the parole denials, and the forever fear.

Although we are still fighting an uphill battle, we are no longer fighting alone. My email and social media accounts are filled with agencies fighting for justice. They all welcome me, even though my voice does not resonate at rallies and I lag behind at marches. It is gratifying to hear young, strong voices chant, "What do we want? JUSTICE!"

I go into the jails less often than I did. I let my clearance expire for the jails and the prisons.

But still, every December, the week before Christmas, this Jewish girl plays Santa Claus to the children who must endure a visit to the Nassau County Jail.

During the early days of Prison Families Anonymous, we would have Christmas parties in the church that housed our office on Washington Street in Hempstead. They were gala events. We always had one of our ex-cons play Santa for our kids.

Bill Arico, Joan's husband, was our first Santa. Billy later became known for his escape from Riker's Island. He was recaptured after about two years, but he died trying to escape from The Metropolitan Correctional Center, a Federal Detention Center in New York City.

People came from all over to enjoy the festivities. I remember the year that two Cadillacs pulled up to the door, with the drivers ready to load the trunks of their cars with our toys. No, no, no. these toys were for our kids. No fear. The gang of good guys, mostly fresh out of prison, limited the amount of swag.

There were always plenty of donated toys, food, and fun. But, I digress.

When my friend, and partner in criminal justice (I almost said "partner in crime") Sue Jones worked for the Office of Prison Ministry of the Diocese of Rockville Centre, she organized the toy distribution at the Suffolk County Jails in Riverhead and Yaphank. For years, Sue would run back and forth between the jails, dropping toys off and assuring herself that there was enough coverage for all visiting hours. Scheduling who would be at which jail during which visiting session was difficult. Our volunteers looked forward to being at the jail to change tears and apprehension into smiles and hope, so they usually were reliable. If not, Sue would scurry about to get someone to cover for them. We couldn't disappoint the children.

Sue is retired from the Office of Prison Ministry. New Hour for Women and Children has taken on the responsibility of providing toys for the children visiting the Suffolk County jails.

THIRTY-SIX
Herstory (2010-2017)

Writing my book was always something I would do "someday." I thought about it, talked about it, and knew that I would get it out there "someday." I had no doubt that the story in my head was interesting and I even spoke to people about ghost writing it with me.

I hoped that someday my story would be told, but I could not picture myself sitting down and actually writing it. It had been years since I had written anything that wasn't required of me. I barely had the patience to write a letter. Strangely, my childhood dream was to be a writer. I filled many composition books with poems and stories I wrote. As a senior in Hempstead High School, I was one of the few students chosen to participate in a creative writing class. Mr. Murphy, my teacher, predicted that one day I would be a successful writer.

That was a world and a lifetime ago.

Fortuitously, Erika Duncan, the founder of Herstory, came into my life. Herstory is a nonprofit organization that "gives voice to people who traditionally have not been heard."

Erika attended a Prison Families Anonymous meeting, hoping to encourage some of our families to attend one of her writing workshops. "Wow," I thought. "Too bad that

I am not ready to sit down and write that book that is still floating around in my head."

Few of our families responded to the opportunity to tell their stories, but a seed was planted within me.

Serena was one who decided to take advantage of Erika's invitation and started writing her memoir with Herstory. "Good for you," I thought. "The world needs to hear your story."

The world heard much more than Serena's story. Serena joined the staff of Herstory and quickly took on a position of leadership. She became the and, with Erika, she has accelerated the goal of using these narratives as a vehicle for change. The world is now being exposed to volumes of stories written by the disenfranchised, the poor, the immigrant, the incarcerated, and the abused. Because their voices are being heard by the decision-makers, these stories are impacting policy and informing social justice decisions.

Through Serena I learned that Herstory had brought a writing workshop to the women in the DWI pod at the Suffolk County jail. The women were being encouraged to find the words to change minds and hearts by telling their stories.

Serena invited me to attend an introductory workshop at the Riverhead Library. I was curious about this innovative jail project. Once I learned that the Suffolk County corrections officers who championed this project would be in attendance, it didn't take much coaxing to get me there.

I invited some members of PFA to join me, and a carload of families and formerly incarcerated people took the forty-five minute drive. Everyone in the car had experienced going into that jail, either in handcuffs or as a visitor. Either way, there was no feeling of nostalgia. We kept right on going and soon the jail was in the rearview mirror.

We eventually found ourselves in the library, sitting in a circle with some citizens, a few activists, and a handful of Suffolk County corrections officers. The enthusiasm of that group was contagious. The officers who worked in the DWI pod were true believers, and they were cheerleaders for the women in this innovative program.

Erika challenged each of us to think of where we might want the "stranger reader" to meet us and then to find the words that would entice that person to want to read our stories. That was the moment I started writing this book. I joined the writers in the Patchogue Writing for Justice workshop and decided that this was now my "someday."

Herstory led me down other paths. I went into the jail with Erika and, through their writing, I got to know these women who were suffering the consequences of the bad choices they had made. They wrote from their hearts and through their written words, they were able to share their common humanity—something rarely seen in a jail. They listened and offered each other encouragement. They wrote about their children, their addictions, and their abuse. Some had been trafficked, some had caused harm to others, but most had suffered unimaginable harm themselves. How brave they were to tell these stories in this setting, despite the fear of being judged again, this time by their peers. With the permission of the women, Erika brought their stories out of confinement and into the hearts of readers.

My meeting with Erika next led to collaboration with PFA, Herstory, and Rachel Wiener, director of the Center for Peace at Central Islip High School. This joint venture led to the publication of a book, *All I Ever Wanted: Stories of the Children of the Incarcerated*. We met with a group of students from the high school, most with a parent incarcerated. The school bused Tanasha, Malaysia, Nicole, Antisha, Aysha, Destiny, and Desmond to Touro Law Center, where these high-school students met in a conference room to talk about their hopes, fears, and dreams. They went home to put these thoughts into stories that were honest and insightful. They shared what they had written at the next week's workshop. We were usually joined by law students and staff who, of course, participated by writing and reading their own stories.

Last year I was at the InterNational Prisoners Family Conference and was quite impressed as I listened to Nkechi, a keynote speaker, talk about how she dealt with the incarceration of her father. She was a beautiful young woman who was the current winner of the Miss Africa Texas title. I was very moved by Nkechi's story; after she spoke, I went to congratulate her on her excellent presentation. I offered her a copy of our folio edition of *All I Ever Wanted: Stories of the Children of the Incarcerated*. She graciously accepted the book and turned to accept accolades from her many admirers. She quickly left the conference to return to school, and I thought no more about it.

Almost a full year later I received a phone call from

Nkechi. She explained that she was entering a worldwide pageant and she asked permission to use this book as her platform.

What an exciting achievement for the children who faced their insecurities and shared their innermost secrets so that their stories could be told!

I recently accepted an invitation to join the Board of Directors of Herstory.

THIRTY-SEVEN
Current Events

I speak whenever and wherever I'm invited. David often reminds me that I should ask for an honorarium when I speak; I reply that I thought I should pay them to hear me.

I particularly like to speak to college students who are considering careers in criminal justice.

I serve on the steering committee of the InterNational Prisoners Family Conference. Hundreds of amazing people convene each year at a hotel in Dallas, Texas, and work creatively to better conditions for the prison family and to put a spotlight on criminal-justice issues around the world. At last count eleven countries were represented.

Attendees from other nations are aghast at some of our country's policies, especially as we criticize other nations for human rights violations: the use of the death penalty, solitary confinement, and the length of our sentences, to name a few. These are no longer tolerated in most other countries.

Among our accomplishments are a drafting of a Coalition White Paper, a Prisoner Family Bill of Rights, a student justice forum, and an international coalition.

A documentary, *Faces of Mass Incarceration*, was filmed during the 2016 conference. It was a collage featuring many of us who have been affected by the scourge of our country's fascination with punishment and revenge.

The conference is spearheaded by my now-friend Carolyn Esparza, the coauthor of *The Unvarnished Truth of the Prison Family Journey.*

Speaking of films, my big screen debut was an appearance in *Walking through Purgatory,* a film inspired by Michael Spaccarotella, whose family was impacted by the incarceration of one of his sons. It is a strong and poignant reminder of how addiction leads to crime, which leads to prison, which leads to the implosion of a middle-class suburban family.

I do utilize some modern technology. If you log onto my Facebook page you will see that I share some life events and family pictures, but you are more apt to see posts lamenting the ways of the world, particularly as it relates to unlawful parole decisions, prosecutorial misconduct, mistreatment of persons with mental illness, overuse of solitary confinement, the death penalty, privatization of prisons, and so on.

As I think that it might be about time to retire, I wonder what it would be like not to have a stack of inmate letters waiting to be answered, conference calls at dinner time, phone calls to return, or meetings to attend. I'm not sure I will ever find out.

I have very vivid dreams every bloody night. My body is so tense that sometimes I feel that I might break in half, but I take deep breaths, stretch, and do my life one day at a time. I hope that my grandchildren remain unscathed. I know the statistics and cannot help but shudder at the thought that Gene's genes might spring up in a future generation.

I have received many accolades and acknowledgments.

But I did not choose to be a do-gooder. I was handed this life. If someone had told me as I walked into Louie's Bar that night in 1963 that "this will be your life, Barbara Pugatz," I would have run like hell. Or would I?

When I look at Tina and Brenda, I thank Gene for my two daughters. If you were a diamond in the rough, dear Gene, the diamonds shone through in our daughters.

EPILOGUE

It is now 2017. Fifty years ago I entered the visiting room of a facility for the very first time. I held my breath and moved robot-like through the process. When Gene was sentenced to "hard time," so was I. I gingerly took little steps to orient myself to this new reality. But just when I thought, "Aha, I got it now. This is how it is," I found that no, something was askew. What was perfectly clear yesterday was now hazy. The rules kept changing for no apparent reason. I felt like Alice in Wonderland slipping down the rabbit hole, where all reality was distorted, nothing was as it seemed, and I was immersed in a world without logic. And the truly frightening, inexplicable part of this story is that it is still this way.

What is down in that huge hole known as the Department of Corrections?

In that world, putting mentally incompetent people into small dark cells for twenty-three hours a day is considered normal.

Yes, that is what we do in 2017. We are doing it to Nikko as I write this. Nikko's diagnosis is dual: addiction and bipolar disorder. When he was seventeen, he committed a nonviolent crime, was arrested, and was sent to prison in the fine state of Florida. Lo and behold, he was not able to adapt. They labeled him noncompliant. As punishment they put him into a tiny room with a cot and a toilet bowl, where he decompensated, sat in a corner in a near-catatonic state. Even though he cannot understand what is happening to him, he is told that he is still being noncompliant. To make this more deplorable, they are denying his mother visitation. That is what we do to mentally ill young people in this rabbit hole.

You want more? Steven Garafolo has been locked up for forty-two years. The judge set his minimum at twenty-five years. You do the math. He has done everything in his power to repent for his crime. He has earned respect and accolades from his keepers and his peers. He has not had a recent institutional infraction, but he is being held because of the nature of the crime, something that will never change, although he certainly has. His sister, one of the few family members still alive, is waiting inside that rabbit hole, hoping for a glimpse of compassion.

I have been to the funerals of many parents whose worst fear came true: "What if I die before my child is released?"

Joe has been in prison for about thirty-five years. As I write this, he is in a prison hospice with stage-4 cancer. He recently suffered a heart attack. His prognosis is not good. Maybe he will live another month or two. He has a wife, children, and grandchildren. They would be willing to bring him home, where his family could have the comfort of being with him as they say their final good-byes. But we are a society where revenge trumps logic. So the taxpayers of New York are footing the bill for not only his medical care but for his custody and control.

I sat by and watched as Lori's beloved husband died alone in a prison hospital, while her heart was hurting because she could not be there with him. Her sentence ended the day he died. To make this even more tragic, Lori remains convinced that her husband was wrongly convicted.

These are not isolated stories.

Because of mandatory minimums and archaic parole practices, our aging prison population is exploding. I correspond with Richard, a man who has been in state prison for more than fifty years. His crime was horrific, but it was committed while he was under the influence of drugs. To this day he has absolutely no memory of the event. Today he is a gentle old man, not capable of hurting anyone, but he is still being held captive. I do not condone any of the crimes, but I wonder when enough is enough. So many of the incarcerated are no longer dangers to society. They are a bunch of old men, gobbling up taxpayer dollars.

In this crazy world, it is *normal* to warehouse people in forensic hospitals, where they are kept locked up without treatment to alleviate the conditions that brought them there in the first place. Charles has been civilly committed for about ten years now. His mother and father came to Prison Families Anonymous twenty-five years ago. Charles was in prison for a rape. When his sentence was completed, he was not allowed back into the community but instead placed in an institution where he was supposed to get treatment. During the years he was in prison, no treatment was ever offered. Treatment was to begin in this forensic hospital where he can be held indefinitely, waiting for the promised programs. Meanwhile, Charles' father died and his mother is in a nursing home. Charles languishes in Central New York Psychiatric Center, losing all hope that treatment will ever be offered. Perhaps he will die waiting.

AJ is in a similar situation. Seventeen years ago, as a teenager, he committed a nonviolent crime, and he pled not guilty by reason of insanity. Had he gone to trial on this charge, he would have been home years ago. His mother has no idea when they will let him out of the forensic hospital on isolated Wards Island, where she goes to visit him at least once a week.

Oh, did I mention *parole?* Of course I did. But it is worth mentioning again and again. Hardly a day goes by that I don't get a call from a family member or a letter from a prisoner asking what they can do to increase the possibility of getting a fair parole hearing. I have to say that, in my humble but educated opinion, there is no such thing as a fair parole hearing. It is a crapshoot. There is no rhyme or reason to who will get parole release and who will not. To add insult to injury, in many states, including New York, parole hearings are conducted via video. It is impersonal and deliberately geared to keep the prison population at a level that will ensure the continuation of the multimillion dollar prison industry, which prospers by its failure.

Of course, I have seen the successes—Glenn, David, Doug, Danny, Joey, Serena, Marie, and so many more—who have been reunited with their families and thrive as taxpaying citizens. Serena has recently been appointed executive director of New Hour for Women and Children–LI. I have been invited to homecoming parties, weddings, graduation parties, and baby showers.

Both of my daughters are successes. Despite statistical predictions, they are both in stable loving marriages. The only interactions they have had with the law were positive. Tina retired as a sergeant in the NYPD. Brenda is established in the corporate world. I have three grandchildren, Aaron, Darien, and Emma. All are good, solid people. Aaron graduated from college with a degree in criminal justice. Darien started college this year, and Emma is a bright preteen. The cycle has been broken.

I write this book to celebrate prison families all over the world, we who never committed a crime but have been sentenced to a prison of our own.

I continue my advocacy work, my speaking engagements, and our support group meetings, all because almost fifty years ago my friend David Rothenberg told me that, if I am not part of the solution, I am part of the problem.

I hope I have been part of the solution.

FAMILY PHOTOS

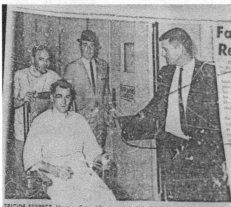

TOP: Gene Allan at the time of his arrest. BOTTOM: Gene and me in happier times, shortly before he was diagnosed with cancer.

PATRICIDE SUSPECT. Herman Gene Allan, accused of the fatal shooting of his father, Hempstead, is wheeled out of the prison ward at Meadowbrook Hospital yesterday escorted by two detectives. The policemen and hospital attendants were unidentified.

TOP: David Rothenberg and me, celebrating David's birthday at Castle Gardens in NYC. BOTTOM: Susan W and Shirley C representing Prison Families Anonymous at a reentry job fair.

TOP: Kenny Jackson and Tina in the backyard at 10 Foster Place. BOTTOM: Me with Bobby Moore, innovator of the Drug Alcohol Rehabilitation Treatment (DART) program at the Nassau County Correctional Center.

TOP: Cover photo of Tina, Gene, me, and Brenda. Taken at Greenhaven Correctional Facility in 1972. BOTTOM: Tina and Brenda show that you can break the cycle.

APPENDIX

The information we provide to those wishing to form a
prison family support group

Prison Families Anonymous, Inc..

pfa.longisland@gmail.com   www.pfa-li.com

631-943-0441

Prison Families Anonymous is a self-help organization whose purpose is to help the families and friends who now have, once had, or are about to have a loved one involved in the criminal or juvenile justice system. PFA began in February of 1974 because three women were concerned about the impact on the family when a loved one becomes involved in the system. It was the hope and intent of the founders to provide a way to keep families from facing their fears and trauma alone.

Our groups meet regularly so members can share their experiences, feelings, hopes, and resources with each other. For meeting schedules, times, and locations, please see our website. Telephone support is available at all times. PFA members give each other support and caring where otherwise there might be none. The confidentiality and anonymity of families is respected at all times.

When the call comes that someone you love has been arrested, a feeling of hopelessness and panic sets in. What is arraignment? Where will s/he sleep tonight? What about a lawyer? Where will the money come from? Why doesn't the lawyer call back? When and how can I visit? Can I bring anything? How will I visit an upstate prison? How can I afford this? Will s/he change while away? Will I? What will I say if my neighbors or friends ask me where s/he is? What do I do or say when the children come home and tell me they were harassed in school? How can I hold my head up if the story was in the newspapers? What do I do about a car, insurance, bills, and the house? Will things be better or worse when s/he comes home? How can I help things improve? How can I learn to trust again?

Most everyone involved in PFA has or once had a friend or loved one arrested, tried, and sentenced to jail or prison. PFA members know what it feels like to love someone accused of a crime. There are agencies and organizations to help formerly incarcerated persons or victims but there is very little available in the way of support for families. PFA fills this vital need. Society accuses, ostracizes, and sentences a family member or friend at the same time as the offender. A wife leaves the courtroom after her husband is sentenced, goes home, looks around, and the reality that she has to go it alone hits her. How will she bring up the children? What will she tell them? How will she feed, clothe, and provide for them? How does she cope with the loneliness? A spouse or parent often examines her or his life and asks what s/he could have done differently. And would doing things differently have prevented the crime? The family knows in their hearts that <u>they</u> are not guilty, yet they feel others pointing the accusing finger. Relatives say to forget him or her. Neighbors can't wait to talk about it.

In addition to providing emotional support, PFA educates families about the criminal justice system, about jails and prisons, about reentry issues, about pending legislation, about resources they may not be aware of. Information is empowering and families need to know that they do have a voice in how the system operates.

PFA cares. PFA is committed to helping strengthen those families who are "doing time on the outside." PFA feels that the family has been sadly neglected. PFA is dedicated to creating awareness, in the system, of the family and its needs, to filling the gap between the arrest and the eventual release back into the community. PFA believes that the family is a valuable and vital resource for preventing recidivism. Strengthening the family serves to strengthen the offender, both during incarceration and after release.

Self-Help Meeting Procedures

This recipe is for all participants to be mindful of. It assures that each of us takes responsibility for our meetings and that regardless of who attends, there is always a facilitator.

1. It is a good idea to decide upon a facilitator for a one-month term

2. Choose a person to read this opening:

Welcome to Prison Families Anonymous. We hope here you will find the help and friendship we are privileged to enjoy. We are a group of relatives and friends who now have or have had a loved one involved in the criminal or juvenile justice system. PFA has but one goal: helping families during this difficult time. We offer each other support and caring where otherwise they may be none.

We understand, as few others can, what it is like to have a loved one arrested, tried, or taken from us. At this time many of us feel helpless, frightened, confused, or lonely.

We come together to share our experiences and talk about our feelings. Through the understanding we have for each other, we try to find the strength to deal with our

problems. By helping ourselves first, we learn that we are better able to help our loved ones. Without such help, living with these problems can be too much for most of us. We offer no solutions, only suggestions.

Because we are an anonymous organization, everything said at meetings or member to member must be held in the strictest confidence. Only by respecting each other's anonymity can we feel free to say what is on our minds and in our hearts.

Will all who care to join me in saying the Serenity Prayer:

God, grant me the serenity to accept the things I cannot change.

The courage to change those things I can,

And the wisdom to know the difference.

3. Go around the room and introduce yourselves by first name only.

4. The group should decide on a meeting topic to be carried over from the previous meeting.

5. The facilitator will ask, "Does anyone have something they want to share?" (Newcomers may need additional time to talk. PFA members should be encouraged to offer their phone numbers or time during the coffee break or after the meeting to assist the newcomers.)

Go around the group and give everyone an opportunity to contribute. It may be too difficult to answer specific prison-related questions as well as to acknowledge the personal feelings of those attending the meeting. Too much time spent answering questions about the system doesn't provide enough opportunity to share and unburden those who have attended previous meetings. The focus then shifts from the person in the group to the one in prison. You might want to devote a specific time during the break for special questions.

The emphasis should be on feelings of self. There should be a nonjudgmental attitude, anonymity, and confidentiality. There should be acceptance of that which cannot be changed and an ability to look at what can be changed (within ourselves and in our situation).

6. The facilitator needs to keep track of the time and skillfully keep participants on point and provide enough time for all to air their feelings. Suggest an exchange of phone numbers among individuals for follow-up phone contact.

7. Pass a basket for donations for the meeting "kitty." Each gives what they can and the money is used for postage or emergencies or refreshments.

8. Ask someone to read the closing:

In closing we would like to say that the opinions expressed here were strictly those of the person who expressed them. Take what you like and leave the rest.

The things you heard were spoken in confidence and should be treated as confidential. Keep them within the walls of this room and the confines of your mind.

A few special words to those of you who haven't been with us long. Whatever your problems, there are those among us who have had them too. If you try to keep an open mind, you will find help. You will come to realize that there is no situation too difficult to be bettered and no unhappiness too great to be lessened.

We aren't perfect. The welcome we gave you may not show the warmth we have in our hearts for you. After a while you'll discover that although you may not like all of us, you'll love us in a very special way, the same way we already love you.

Talk to each other. Reason things out with someone else. But let there be no gossip or criticism of one another. Instead, let the understanding, love, and peace of our group grow in you one day at a time.

And please come back.

Group Ground Rules

1. *Be responsible for your own learning.*

Do not wait to be asked to participate. The more effort you put into the group, the more personal learning you will experience.

2. *Accept others as they are.*

This is done by accepting what others say and by not judging or correcting. It is possible to like a person and not like or agree with what they say or do.

3. *Avoid put-downs.*

Avoid putting yourself or others down. To enable you to honestly evaluate your personal strengths is the first step in looking at self and relating that information to the world of work.

4. *You have the option to pass.*

A large part of this program is making you aware of the many choices that are available. In the group each person has the right to pass if s/he feels unwilling to share. It is okay to say "I pass" for you do not have to participate.

5. *Group confidentiality is a must.*

For trust to exist and for personal growth to occur, whatever is said or shared in the group stays in the group.

6. *Expect unfinished business.*

The group provides a "how to" process. Members are learning how to value, make meaningful decisions, make career and life choices. This group will introduce ideas, situations, and/or issues that do not have any clear-cut answers. Group members' values will probably not all be the same and some members may reach clearer and faster decisions than others. This is to be expected.

Ten Tips for Families

Choose to take charge of your life and don't let your loved one's incarceration always take center stage.

Remember to be good to yourself. Love, honor, and value yourself. You're doing a very hard job and you deserve some quality time just for you.

Watch out for signs of depression and don't delay in getting professional help when you need it.

If people offer to help, accept the offer and suggest specific things they can do.

Educate yourself about your loved one's incarceration. Information is empowering.

There is a difference between caring and doing. Be open to ideas.

Trust your instincts. Most of the time they'll lead you in the right direction.

Grieve for your losses and then allow yourself to dream new dreams.

Stand up for your rights as the family.

Seek support from others in the same situation. There is great strength in knowing you are not alone.

(Taken from 1998 National Family Caregivers Association)

Five Coping Styles of Families of the Incarcerated

Note that there are factors that impact the family's ability to cope and that there are some coping styles that families use. Even within these styles there are differences.

- The <u>families on hold</u> freeze-frame their lives. They write, telephone, and try to involve the incarcerated person as much as possible. They try to make the period of incarceration OK. They do not talk about the feelings, the anger, and they rarely talk about the crime. They are often in denial but keep going.

- The <u>parallel family</u> has a more realistic point of view. They keep in touch but they have a "life goes on" attitude, with each person growing on separate tracks. The incarcerated person may be getting their GED. The person on the outside may be learning to balance the checkbook. The children are developing skills and interests, too.

- In the <u>estranged family</u> the incarcerated person may want to "do the time and not let the time do me." This may mean that contact with the family will be too much to bear. The family on the outside may feel that this crime or this incarceration is the last straw and they want to cut off communication in order to cope.

- The <u>turbulent family</u> is in constant turmoil. They may have contact but it is often filled with anger and can include harsh and abusive interactions.

- The fifth family type is the rarest. They are open and communicating about the crime, the impact on family members, and how they are growing. They are the <u>functioning family</u>.

Obstacles to Parent-Child Visits in Prison

➢ Inadequate information about visiting procedures

➢ Difficulty scheduling visits

➢ Geographic location of prison facilities

➢ Family's inability to afford transportation

➢ Visiting procedures that are uncomfortable or humiliating

➢ Visiting rooms that are inhospitable to children

➢ Foster parents or caregivers who are unwilling to facilitate visits

Source: Women's Prison Association. *When a Mother is Arrested: How the Criminal Justice and Child Welfare Systems Can Work Together More Effectively*. Baltimore, Maryland Department of Human Resources, 1996.

Typical Feelings of Children of Prisoners

Fear – Children are afraid of being abandoned, of never seeing their incarcerated parent again, and of being taken away from the caregiver.

Worry – Concerns about the wellbeing of the incarcerated parent are common, even when the child's relationship with that parent was troubled. Children also worry that their caregivers will not be able to take care of them, that there will not be enough food or money.

Confusion – Often children are not told the truth about their parent's whereabouts. This leads to questions that children are afraid to ask and confusion around what is true and what is not.

Sadness – All of these feelings are ultimately about loss. All loss raises old loss and so for children who have experienced loss of their parents prior to the incarceration, through divorce, drugs, rehab programs, and separate living arrangements, this loss triggers all the pain of previous loss.

Guilt – Children often feel responsible for their parent's behavior. They wish they had tried harder to stop the parent's drug use, blame themselves for not getting better grades or not cleaning their rooms, and suffer the guilt of not being "enough" of a motivation for changing parental behavior.

Isolation – There is a conspiracy of silence that is often expected of children in families of prisoners. Social stigma and new surroundings keep children from talking to peers. Well-intentioned caregivers, who attempt to distract and protect children from distress, may avoid conversations about the parent and the circumstances, leaving the child to feel very alone.

Embarrassment and Stigma – Children with parents in jail or prison feel stigmatized even when they live in communities where many people have family and friends who are incarcerated. Some children even appear to be boastful as they defend against the pain and embarrassment.

Anger – Anger is a secondary emotion. It usually comes in the wake of other feelings, such as disappointment, resentment, frustration, fear, or loss.

All of these feelings and the anger that often accompanies them are typical for children of prisoners.

What feelings did this list raise for you? Which feeling surprise you? Worry you? Make you feel sad or angry? Identify how knowing these feelings will impact the [way in which you deal with the children of prisoners].

—Mentoring Children of Prisoners

Prison Family Bill of Rights

*As affirmed at the 2012 National Prisoner's Family
Conference
and formally adopted at the 2013 National Prisoner's Family
Conference*

The Prison Family has the Right to be treated with respect and dignity by any and all representatives of the prison system at all times.

The Prison Family has the Right to expect and be assured the utmost care is established and maintained to provide a healthy and safe living environment that promotes effective rehabilitation, reintegration, and parole planning throughout a loved one's incarceration.

The Prison Family has the Right to be treated as and integrated as a positive resource in the process of rehabilitation and reintegration and parole planning of an incarcerated loved one.

The Prison Family has the Right to receive consistency in the enforcement of rules, regulations, and policies affecting a loved one's incarceration.

The Prison Family has the Right to receive consistency in the enforcement of rules, regulations, and/or policies affecting visitation and/or all forms of communication with an incarcerated loved one.

The Prison Family has the Right to be informed in a timely, clear, forthright, and respectful manner of any changes in rules, regulations, and/or policies affecting visitation and/or communication with an incarcerated loved one.

The Prison Family has the Right to be informed within 24 hours and in a compassionate manner regarding the illness, injury, and/or death of an incarcerated loved one.

The Prison Family has the Right to extended visitation during the hospitalization of an incarcerated loved one.

The Prison Family has the Right to be informed within 24 hours of the security status change and/or transfer of an incarcerated loved one to a new facility.

The Prison Family has the Right to be provided specific written and evidence-based reasons for a loved one's security change, clemency denial, or parole denial.

The Prison Family has the Right to have their incarcerated loved one housed within a distance from their permanent address that provides reasonable access for visitation and/or to facilitate serving as a resource in the rehabilitation and reintegration preparation and parole planning of their incarcerated loved one.

The Prison Family has the Right to be provided the current specific name of names and direct phone numbers of prison officials to contact for questions about their incarcerated loved one.

The term "Prison Family" is herein defined as including, but not limited to, a blood or adopted relation, spouse, domestic partner, and/or trusted friend designated by an incarcerated person upon or during a period of confinement as one who will serve as an outside contact on his or her behalf for the relaying of any communication regarding the medical and mental health, security status and location of the incarcerated person, and/or for making critical decisions on behalf of the incarcerated person in the event of his or her incapacitation.

CPSIA information can be obtained
at www.ICGtesting.com
Printed in the USA
LVHW051110200119
604573LV00018B/693/P